国际和平城市
丛书
International Cities of Peace

国家出版基金项目
江苏省"十四五"重点图书出版规划项目
侵华日军南京大屠杀遇难同胞纪念馆资助项目

德国
德累斯顿

DRES-DEN

Germany

International Cities of Peace

Series Editor: Liu Cheng
Associate Editors: Ling Xi   Chen Junfeng

Egon Spiegel   **Translated by Nikolas Michael Krause**

南京师范大学出版社

United Nations Educational, Scientific and Cultural Organization

UNESCO Chair on Peace Studies
Nanjing University
People's Republic of China

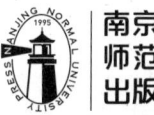

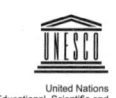

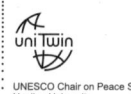

图书在版编目（CIP）数据

德国·德累斯顿 =Dresden, Germany：英文 /（德）埃贡·施皮格尔（Egon Spiegel）著；（美）罗克（Nikolas Michael Krause）译 . -- 南京：南京师范大学出版社，2022.8
（国际和平城市丛书 / 刘成主编）
ISBN 978-7-5651-5348-8

Ⅰ . ①德… Ⅱ . ①埃… ②罗… Ⅲ . ①德累斯顿—概况—英文 Ⅳ . ①K951.65

中国版本图书馆CIP数据核字（2022）第115794号

丛 书 名	国际和平城市丛书
丛书主编	刘　成
丛书副主编	凌　曦　陈俊峰
书　　名	Dresden, Germany
著　　者	［德］埃贡·施皮格尔（Egon Spiegel）
译　　者	［美］罗克（Nikolas Michael Krause）
策划编辑	徐　蕾　郑海燕
责任编辑	王　嘉
书籍设计	瀚清堂
出版发行	南京师范大学出版社
地　　址	江苏省南京市玄武区后宰门西村9号（邮编：210016）
电　　话	（025）83598712（编辑部）83598919（总编办）83598412（营销部）
网　　址	http://press.njnu.edu.cn
电子信箱	nspzbb@njnu.edu.cn
照　　排	南京私书坊文化传播有限公司
印　　刷	上海雅昌艺术印刷有限公司
开　　本	889毫米×1194毫米　1/32
印　　张	10.125
版　　次	2022年8月第1版　2022年8月第1次印刷
书　　号	ISBN 978-7-5651-5348-8
定　　价	50.00元
出 版 人	张志刚

* 南京师大版图书若有印装问题请与销售商调换
* 版权所有　侵犯必究

Foreword by Series Editor

This book series, International Cities of Peace, Volume I, introduces five cities, which have one thing in common that they have all experienced the trauma of war in their history, and the collective memories have endured from one generation to the next. So, history must be kept in mind. Only by looking back on past sufferings and using history as a mirror can we prevent such historical tragedies from occurring again. It is absolutely vital to recognize and remember the historical trauma, but how we remember it may affect its authenticity and how long we will keep it in mind. According to history, building peace is the best remedy for remembering and recovering from the past suffering. When the traumatic memory of a city is transformed into a common human memory, we can understand the past disasters in a new way beyond stereotyped political memory. Only this can enable the traumatic history to be linked to the future peace, which can promote the reconciliation between the former hostile parties, and boost hope to the establishment of a community with a shared future for mankind. History indicates that reconciliation means not only exchanging our views and experiences of the past, but also a process of mutually creating new ideas for the future and sharing new experiences. In this way, reconciliation is a thought and a power that meets our mutual needs, which can be developed by building cities of peace with the legacy bequeathed by the war. That is why we wrote these books.

All the five cities of the book series are actively engaged in building a culture of peace. Nanjing, the first International City of Peace in China, held an international peace forum on positive peace; Dresden reflects on the war experience of Germany and strengthens domestic and international reconciliation; Hiroshima leads non-governmentally the anti-nuclear peace movement in Japan; Warsaw promotes the reconciliation dialogue that has led to a shared historical memory both inside and outside Poland; Coventry is the benchmark for British reconciliation. At the same time, the study of war memory is undergoing changes in three dimensions: shifts from the hero memory to the traumatic memory, from the memory of a victorious country to the memory of all the wounded countries, and from the domestic historical memory of a country to historical memory shared by many countries. Our belief is that the memory of war will be ultimately eclipsed by the memory of peace, as more and more cities work towards building cities of peace and thus form a global network of peace cities.

The five cities have their own characteristics in building a city of peace. Their practice of building peace has proven the truth that "There is no way to peace; peace is the way". Cities of peace all share a common purpose, promoting the culture of peace advocated by UNESCO, that is, working to build peace through conflict prevention, mediation and transformation; providing peace education on non-violence, tolerance, acceptance, respect and sustainable development; promoting intercultural dialogue and reconciliation. To build a city of peace requires the joint efforts of governments, universities, social groups, non-government organizations and citizens from all countries and regions around the world, for it needs to incorporate elements of peace in historical records, memories and heritage. It can be achieved in many ways, such as conflict prevention, peace-keeping, peace-building, peace research, peace education, and all peace activities that promote urban progress and prosperity as well as world peace and development.

This book series rests on its disciplinary foundation, Peace Studies. With the only UNESCO Chair on Peace Studies in China, Nanjing University is widely recognized as the center of China's Peace Studies. The development of China's Peace Studies has received great help from many institutions and individuals around the world. Without their support, Peace Studies would not have developed in China, and these books would not have been published, either. This book series took ten years to compile, experiencing ups and downs along the way, and finally came out. All the authors, translators and editors have done their best to bring out these books against all the odds, and make them authentic, scholarly, innovative, and readable at the same time.

This book series is an attempt to understand how cultural trauma and historical memory affect us. We sincerely welcome readers to point out and correct the defects and mistakes in these books.

Liu Cheng

Professor, School of History, Nanjing University

Chairholder of UNESCO Chair on Peace Studies

August 2022

Preface

In the summer of 2011, I was able to show my colleague Prof. Liu Cheng and his wife, He Lan the sights of a city in Germany that not so long ago, and in some places still today, was or is clearly marked by the consequences of World War II: Dresden. Since I was able to take up my first professorship there at the turn of the millennium, I have special ties to this city. During our visits, which included a visit to the Technical University of Dresden and many of the city's sights, as well as the search for evidence of the destruction caused by World War II and the reconstruction, many parallels between what happened to the people of Nanjing during the occupation of their city by Japanese invaders in 1937-1938 and what Dresden had to endure in terms of destruction on February 13 to 15, 1945, as a result of the bombing by British-American bomber units, came to our attention. Despite all the differences between a massacre like the one in Nanjing and a bombing like the one in Dresden, as well as their specific military or political backgrounds, there is one thing they have in common: the unspeakable suffering of the population as a result of war, as well as the survivors and their descendants coping with or coming to terms with the experience. Still in Dresden, we decided to devote ourselves to the deconstruction of the two cities against the background of their previous heyday and their reconstruction, each in its own, comparable studies. It was obvious that in this context we would not be able to avoid devoting our attention to "Coventry" and "Hiroshima"—they, too, epitomize spatial destruction. After Liu Cheng and I visited Warsaw together, it was clear to us that we would also have to include this city, which was destroyed by up to 80% in World War II, in our project.

But then do Stalingrad and Guernica not also deserve—even special—consideration? And what about the many other cities, among them those that were comparatively (in percentage terms) even more severely hit by the war than those that, for whatever reason, became symbols of the destructive power of World War II, such as Coventry and Dresden? Thanks to the commitment of amateur researchers—at least in Germany—the extent of the destruction caused by the past world war and the achievements of reconstruction even in many smaller towns, are being recorded more or less systematically. As such, a considerable basis for commemorating the war in particular and in general, as well as for appreciating the way its consequences were dealt with locally, has been created.

What would the retrospective be without perspective? In this volume and in the other volumes, we do not want to lament and accuse alone in retrospect of war. We want to capture and reflect at least parts of the dynamic that grips people and enables them to defy the paralysis caused by immeasurable destruction and indescribable suffering and to courageously attempt a new beginning out of pure chaos, thus showing that even the worst war can be nothing more than the completely superfluous turning point between construction and reconstruction, between a prosperity before and a prosperity after, which cannot be justified by anything. Destruction, we can learn here, has neither the first nor the last word. It is always only an intermezzo of senseless exuberance and blind wantonness, of hubris. It always lacks rationality, even if it always tries to cloak itself in its political mantle and in this way gains approval. Nor is it an expression of an inherently inevitable disease of an inherently healthy organism. This classification, presented here only in rough sketch, is an essential moment of our reappraisal. War is always a senseless, counterproductive sham. Dresden is a symbol of this general assessment.

This is not a kind of travel guide for Dresden, nor is it another book about Dresden as a victim of war, especially of the bombing in February 1945. Rather, it is a contribution to the question of how Dresden—considering selected examples—productively came to terms with the bombing and, hence, with the war per se in the horizon of its history and its self-image.

Once again, my secretary, Mrs. Gerda Büssing, has provided me with excellent support in my work. This applies not only to the selection of the extensive illustrative pictures, but also and above all to the careful indexing of its individual sources and last but not least the enormously laborious and tedious procurement of printing rights.

Special thanks are also due to the translator of the German edition into English, Dr. Nikolas Michael Krause, Research Affiliate at the UNESCO Chair on Peace Studies, Nanjing University. Dr. Krause not only translated the text within a very short time and under considerable time pressure, but also pointed out unforgivable minor and major errors to the author with regard to the German edition and, in addition, made technical queries to individual passages. Through various clarifications, obvious misunderstandings could be prevented. The publication benefited not only from the translator's specialization as a historian with a doctorate, but also from his biographical bilingualism, i.e. his unrestricted familiarity with the German as well as the English language in its American variant, and last but not least from his existential connection with China and thus with the actual addressees of the present work on the bombing of Dresden on those fateful days and nights in February 1945.

A special gratitude is also extended to the publisher and the editors of the series for making a twofold translation possible. Thus, Dresden as a Memorial of Peace is made accessible to an extremely wide audience through both a Chinese and English translation of the original German edition.

This book is dedicated to the people of the world, especially to children, like Luna Mara Spiegel and Elia Noah Spiegel. May they be spared a "Dresden", and may they do everything in their power to ensure that everyone else is spared such an experience, too.

Egon Spiegel
Nanjing/Vechta

Contents

001

Foreword by Series Editor

004

Preface

010

Introduction

014

Dresden before World War II

History	018
Architecture and Art	023
Location and Surroundings	068
Society	086

098

Dresden in World War II

The Context of War	102
Everyday War Life	142
The February Bombing	149
Symbolization	174

180

Dresden after World War II

Biophilia vs. Extermination	184
Removal of Ruins	188
Reconstruction	191
Politicization of a City	208
Peacebuilding Activities and Measures	219

302

Conclusion

314

Main Bibliography

Introduction

Even though the cities of the former GDR (German Democratic Republic) began to change for the better after the fall of the Berlin Wall and the Iron Curtain at the end of 1989 and so with reuniting Germany, which had been divided into East and West after World War II even a good 30 years after the reunification of the two parts, the gray veil of a visibly hampered development under the conditions of the postwar political era still lies on East Germany and its cities and communities in many cases. Dresden is no exception, although after its "destruction" at the end of World War II, it was and is able to regain its considerable charisma and the splendor of old times has begun to return.

The reconstruction of Church of Our Lady (Frauenkirche), which was largely financed by donations, is more than just symbolic. It is a unique tourist magnet and therefore also highly profitable for the city. In the first two and a half years after its completion alone, it attracted five million visitors. The highly frequented Church of Our Lady not only represents the reconstruction of a city destroyed at its core, but also functions as a widely visible memorial for reconciliation and against war. However, the fate of every single person who fell victim to the historic night of bombing is no less of a reminder for peace.

In Dresden, according to meanwhile secured knowledge, between 22,700 and 25,000 people lost their lives, each one being one too many. The fact that some—for whatever motives—increase the number of those killed contrary to the truth, assume a basically total instead of a partial destruction of the city and try to present the bombing as an incomparable inferno, does not serve the cause at all, i.e. the objective reappraisal of the complex connections in the interest of a condemnation of war that is ultimately as general as it is principled. By emphasizing the bombing of Dresden—out of the multitude of other, comparatively even more heavily hit cities in wartime Germany at the time—the problem of war is punctuated and exclusive and ultimately relativized and reduced in this way. It is encountered in a limited local event, as a result of the bipolar confrontation of a special attacker on the one side (British-American bomber units) and equally a special attack on the other side (Dresden's population). The particular focus is on the British war strategy, which, unlike the American strategy, aims to break the will of the population through an area bombardment that specifically involves the civilian population.

Attempts to commemorate the inferno and to come to terms with the collective trauma, on the other hand, only begin to make sense from a peace education perspective if they take away its uniqueness and place the undoubtedly enormous destruction of the core city in the larger context of war-related or war-induced destruction per se. Dresden is a no more and no less terrible example of devastation by military force. It stands for the many others and for the hostility to life of war in general. The following remarks serve to objectify the sometimes emotionally highly charged debate in the declared interest of an optimal evaluation according to peace studies. With a view to this, not least the National Socialist past of Dresden will have to be illuminated nor the enemy attacks—which are to be understood as counterattacks—that befell Dresden, not only in February 1945, will have to be put into context.

Since the establishment of a commission of historians for the scientific and thus open-ended investigation of the air raids on Dresden in 2004 and 2007, and its final report in 2010, which was eagerly awaited by the public, future research projects can fall back on solid, interdisciplinary research results and—in the course of gaining further knowledge—certainly continue them. In order to obtain reliable data on deaths in connection with the bombing and the number of refugees in Dresden at the time of the air raids, the commission not only conducted thorough research in the Dresden city archives, but also made inquiries at over 800 archives and institutions throughout the Federal Republic of Germany. Thanks to an extensive electronic database, all conceivable evidence of a person's death was collected and recorded, i.e. a total of 57,569 pieces of documented individual information were compiled. An essential, one may say, decisive role in the attempt to gain person-specific evidence was played by research with regard to 31 cemeteries in the Dresden city area, as well as 17 cemeteries in the surroundings of Dresden and the reliability of the (regardless of the war events extremely thorough) information on the burials. The Historical Commission finally determined 1,356,242 documented death declarations throughout Germany and, against the background of registrations in the civil registry, arrived at a figure of approximately 18,000 persons killed by the bombing.

With regard to a maximum number, the Historical Commission—taking into account all only usable sources and on the basis of all only conceivable reflections and interpretations—does not get beyond the maximum number of 25,000 killed. At the same time, the commission never tires of emphasizing that, in view of the commission's mandate, the goal cannot be to establish a number that is reliable down to the one-digit range, but only to establish the order of magnitude within the conflicting field of highly contradictory figures.

When we emphasize in the following the limitation of the destruction caused by the bombardment to the city center in particular, our aim is by no means to minimize the consequences of a military counterstrike that is appalling in terms of both scope and intensity, but to make it clear that military destruction, even where it aims at the broadest possible, if not total, destruction, reaches a limit. Destruction, seen as a whole, does not have the last word. Also, and especially not, in the case of Dresden.

War, whichever one, does not have the last word, however, it announces itself again and again. In particular, in the case of Dresden, this can be illustrated by the fate of the Cross Church (Kreuzkirche). The fact that the church was destroyed a total of five times (it was burned down twice, in 1491 during a big fire in the city and in 1897, and was always rebuilt and restored) shows how we obviously prefer to rotate within the field of tension of construction, destruction and reconstruction, of peace, war and peace. It is not 200 years ago that the church, bombed to ruins in the Seven Years' War in 1760, was hit by another bombardment in 1945. It was burnt out completely and again the reconstruction followed from 1945 to 1955. Shouldn't it have been the last one at least this time? It is hard to imagine that the circular movement will continue. During the time of the "Wende" (reunification of Germany) in 1989-1990, the Cross Church was also a place of protest. To this day, it sees itself as a platform for social reorganization.

The central intention of this volume is to show that war does not have the first nor does it have the last word. This is also the reason why the volume is structured and organized in three steps. It is not a publication that takes an isolated look at Dresden, the historic core of which was destroyed during World War II. It is a volume both about the bombing and about the Dresden before and especially about the Dresden after.

Chapter 1
Dresden before World War II

In order to visualize the consequences of the bombardment of this city steeped in history, its cultural profile in general and its urban planning profile in particular should first be recalled. Here, as in the following, the term "destruction of Dresden" is avoided or always referred to parts of Dresden, because this misleadingly suggests that Dresden as a whole was razed to the ground by the bombings. The Historical Commission speaks here of a "narrative image" that was used, hesitantly at first by German foreign propaganda, and eventually by non-fiction authors and journalists, for decades after 1945. It also had a fact-distorting influence on the memory of contemporary witnesses and the prevailing dimensions of destruction.

When looking back on Dresden's past, it is always right to speak of Dresden as the "Florence on the Elbe". In the architectural and artistic appreciation of Dresden, a parallel is explicitly drawn to Florence, which is highly esteemed from the point of view of art. What Florence is in Italy, Dresden is on the Elbe. The comparison alone indicates how Dresden was perceived in the times before its military destruction, especially with regard to its unique cultural treasures.

A look at Dresden, initially still untroubled by destruction, will also help to understand the not entirely self-evident fact that Dresden, of all places, could become the symbol of wartime destruction—"like Dresden"—or, in the words of Matthias Neutzner, the "cipher for the Allies air war" par excellence and not one of those numerous German cities that were more severely affected in terms of human victims, destroyed urban areas or destroyed buildings (in some cases even unequally).

To begin with, Dresden is the contrast of fascinating beauty of a city on the one hand, its nimbus of a cultural capital, and the deep fall into the dissolution of this beauty, into the unimaginable, basically unexpected, misery of a city destroyed at its core on the other hand. In order to understand this, it is necessary to look at Dresden before its partial military destruction. In doing so, it will inevitably come to light what is usually not or only rarely or not completely taken into consideration, that it actually had to happen the way it did. The bombing of Dresden was basically pre-programmed, so it should not have surprised anyone.

In this context, the formulation that has become so self-evident, that Dresden was bombed just even shortly before the end of World War II, could be discussed in terms of its logic. It is true that, according to historically reliable retrospection, the time of the bombing was indeed shortly before the end of the war, and that at this point in time the end of the war may have (long since) become apparent to many. However, it is questionable whether the war, at the time of the bombing, could already have been considered as ended. The bombing was followed—as we know today—by the imminent end of World War II, but it could have turned out differently. Only against the background of the possibility, which cannot be excluded, that the war could have dragged on for a (much) longer period of time, the aspect that Dresden was bombed even shortly before the end of the war can be neglected. What can be formulated historically in terms of the outcome makes no sense in precisely this formulation ("immediately before the end of the war"): At the time of its execution, the bombing could not have been conceived of in terms of the imminent end of the war, but only as a military-strategic puzzle and justified by those responsible. This neither defuses the fact per se, nor does it make the question superfluous whether it was strategically indicated and appropriate, certainly not the question of its ethical justification.

History

In terms of human history, Dresden's roots go back to the Neolithic Age, and the first major buildings can be traced back to the 5,000 B.C.E. The name Dresden first appears in a document from 1206, and as a city for the first time in 1216. Before that time, Slavic fishermen settled there. The fishing village became a merchant settlement and finally a residence of the Saxon nobility. Around 1500, no more than 6,000 people lived in Dresden. It was not until the early to mid-18th century that the population grew to more than 60,000, and till the mid-19th century, Dresden had more than 100,000 inhabitants. Before that in 1495, Dresden was almost completely destroyed by fire. Dresden was not unaffected by denominational disputes. Although the city was spared from the Thirty Years' War (1618-1648), it was not spared from the plague (so in 1349, 1540 and 1552). The practice of witch hunts, which lasted for three centuries (ca. 1400-1700), is inglorious. Napoleon's battle for Dresden in 1813 led to great destruction. A revolution against the Saxon king enthroned in Dresden in the mid-19th century, the so-called Dresden May Revolution in May 1849, was put down.

According to this, Dresden, as a theater of war, remained spared from wars until World War II, but was affected by World War I, not only by a large number of soldiers who had to give up their lives in World War I or returned home disabled, but also by a catastrophic supply situation no less than that of all other cities and rural areas in Germany. While at the beginning of the war, as it was for many in prewar

Fig.1-1 Dresdeners awaiting the news of mobilization order in front of the newspaper building Dresdener Anzeige on August 1, 1914

Germany, masses in Dresden greatly desired the mobilization order [Fig.1-1], there was a considerable part of the population—in the vicinity of the social-democratic Dresden People's Newspaper (Volkszeitung)—that also took an anti-militarist position. A few days before the outbreak of war, a respectable 35,000 Dresden residents demonstrated against the war.

A generally widespread enthusiasm for the war in Germany, also in Dresden, was soon followed by disillusionment. Among the 10 million people killed in the war, 2 million were Germans. Saxony alone recorded 120,000 soldiers who died in the war and 53,000 people who lost their lives as a result of disease and malnutrition. Among the half of German university professors who had signed a declaration in support of German war policy as late as October 1914 were numerous members of the Technical College of Dresden (TH Dresden) as well as the Veterinarian College in Dresden. Not much later, 322 members of the TH Dresden alone lost their lives.

As Dresden was one of the centers of European politics, especially in the 18th century, it later had the largest art collections in Europe—thanks to sustained support from the electoral court. Despite bitter setbacks caused by plague, and war—it took Dresden more than half a century to get over the destruction of a large part of its urban area by Prussian troops in the mid-18th century—in the 16th and 17th centuries Dresden saw successes in the construction of buildings overall. This, in conjunction with the art collections, owed much to the special interest of the Elector (and, since 1698, the Polish King) Friedrich August I. After Napoleon, industrialization took hold in Dresden. In the late 19th century, Dresden developed into one of the largest garrison cities (with a correspondingly large network of barracks). A few years after the end of World War I and the formation of the Free State of Saxony as a result of the November Revolution in 1918, the city experienced a new cultural flowering with impressive achievements in the artistic field. A highlight of this period was the opening of the Hygiene Museum in 1930.

With the rise of National Socialism, the persecution and extermination of 5,000 Jewish citizens began in Dresden in 1933. The burning of books in 1933 was followed by the confiscation or destruction of cultural assets and the obstruction of theater and opera. In 1938, the Dresden Synagogue was burned down, the city's Jewish residents were mistreated and deported to concentration camps, with their property confiscated. Concentration camps were established in Dresden, and hundreds of women performed forced labor in the armament factories. Between 1933 and 1945, far more than a thousand death sentences, mainly against opponents of the regime, were passed and executed by guillotine in the Dresden District Court.

For centuries—and this is of particular interest and worth emphasizing in the context of this paper—Dresden was a military center where large military units were still being deployed until the end of World War II.

The fact that Dresden was a considerable fortress until the 19th century, with a fortification that had been preserved since the Middle Ages, is reflected by battles for its capture during the Seven Years' War (1756-1763) as well as by the Battle of Dresden [Fig.1-2] in August 1813. According to documents, Dresden had been fortified by a city wall since 1299 at the latest, in reality probably about a century earlier (by a palisade fortification). The fortification was gradually expanded and, for example, a second, lower rampart as well as bastion towers were added. Neuralgic points were the gates. With the invention of black powder and the development of cannons, fortifications had to be designed to withstand massive shelling. From then on, earthen ramparts played a special role in the construction of protective walls. Between 1809 and 1830, Dresden was systematically decomposed under the direction of a demolition commission. The Brühl's Terrace (also known as the "Balcony of Europe") can still be visited as a fortification today. Other parts of the former fortifications are scattered throughout the old and new towns. Under the casemates, vault-like tunnels can still be seen today, in other places bastions with battlements and embrasures.

Fig.1-2 *The Battle of Dresden*, lithography by Antoine Vernet and Jacques Swebach

Not far from Dresden is the Koenigstein Fortress, one of the largest mountain fortresses in Europe. The castle complex of Stolpen, 30 km east of Dresden, is also interesting from the point of view of military history.

In 1998, the Army Officers' School was established in Dresden, as the central training or advanced training facility of the German Armed Forces of 3,500 officer candidates or officers annually. This facility alone shows that the city of Dresden—at least one side of the city—is also currently striving to play a role in the larger context of German military policy. Hence, Dresden thus continues to move in the tradition of a city that strives for relevance in the great military whole and thus—once again—must not rub its eyes in the future when such things hit back at the city on the same level. The intentions and contexts are and remain the same, beyond their respective new interpretations.

Architecture and Art

Because Dresden is largely determined by its architecture and is known worldwide for it, and because this architecture was demonstrably destroyed to a large extent in World War II for all to see, it is to be given special consideration here as a coordinate of the coexistence that was hit at the core by the war.

Church of Our Lady (Protestant) and Dresden Cathedral (Catholic), the Semper Opera House, Royal Palace and Zwinger—to name just a few of their imposing buildings from the Renaissance, Baroque and Wilhelminian periods—stand for a Dresden that enjoys world fame because of the density and uniqueness of its buildings and the art objects they contain, and that for centuries has been and continues to be a center of attractions not only for the aesthetically refined and particularly educated, but also for all those who simply appreciate and, therefore, like to visit beautiful places and who enjoy the appealing surroundings, the ensemble of buildings and the entire ambience of the core city, as well as numerous unique art treasures at least during the moments of their visit. As a city situated on the Elbe, Dresden may rightly have been called "Florence on the Elbe", with reference to the Italian Florence, and today, after extensive reconstruction efforts, it is once again described as such.

Architecture

The architecture that characterizes Dresden's cityscape can understandably only be illustrated by a few significant examples. It should be noted that they only develop their real effect on the viewer in the ensemble and as a whole, i.e. when visited on site. Since, against this background, even the best travel guide cannot be an adequate substitute, an exemplary introduction may suffice here as well. The selection of the objects naturally obeys subjective criteria.

Zwinger [Fig.1-3]: Built at the beginning of the 18th century from 1710 to 1728, under the direction of the architect Matthäus Daniel Pöppelmann and the sculptor Balthasar Permoser, the orangery with its courtly festival square is one of the most imposing buildings of the late Baroque period and represents a "complete work of art consisting of architecture, sculptures and paintings". The reconstruction of this complex, which fell victim to the bombing of Dresden, began immediately after the end of the war. Today, the Old Masters Picture Gallery, the Mathematical-Physical Salon and the Porcelain Collection can be admired here.

Fig.1-3 Wallpavillion of Zwinger

Semper Art Gallery (Die Gemäldegalerie) [Fig.1-4]: It is a museum building designed by Gottfried Semper, built between 1847 and 1854. The gallery building was intended to emulate the Italian High Renaissance. It houses the Old Masters Picture Gallery and a sculpture collection. The building, which was severely damaged during World War II, was extensively restored between 2013 to 2019.

Royal Palace (Residenzschloss): Built at the end of the 15th century and modified several times in the course of different architectural epochs (Romanticism to Historicism), the Royal Palace was rebuilt [Fig.1-5], after its destruction in the war, from 1980 to 1986 and converted into a museum. According to its original function, it served as the seat of power for the Saxon kings and electors. As a museum, it now houses the Historic Green Vault, the New Green Vault, the Cabinet of Copper Engravings, the Coin Cabinet, as well as the Armory and the Turkish Chamber (as one of the world's most important collections of Ottoman art).

Fig.1-4 Semper Art Gallery, view from the inner courtyard of Zwinger to the Gallery

Fig.1-5 Royal Palace

Fig.1-6 Outer view of Semper Opera House, prior to WWII

Semper Opera House (Semperoper) : Named after its architect, Gottfried Semper (1803-1879), the Royal Court and State Opera House was built from 1838 to 1841, in the style of the early Italian Renaissance [Fig.1-6], but was destroyed by fire in 1869. Since Semper had to flee because of his participation in the May Uprisings (also known as the Dresden May Revolution, from May 3 to 9, 1849, aimed to overthrow the Saxon king, Frederick August II, and establish a Saxon republic) and was also denied a return to Saxony after the fire disaster, he created a new design of the Opera House from Vienna. This was realized in 1871-1878 by his son Manfred Semper, a stone's throw away from the Elbe in the historic city center of Dresden but was severely damaged by the bombing of Dresden in 1945. The Opera House, reopened after its faithful restoration in 1977-1985, is one of the most magnificent of its kind in Europe. Approximately 300 events are held there every year, attended by nearly 300,000 guests.

Church of Our Lady (Frauenkirche): This sacral building [Fig.1-7], angular on the outside and round on the inside, is not only one of the most important testimonies to monumental architecture under the conditions of a limited innercity space. It is today, after a moving history, a baroque building with a great peace-political symbolic power. The design for the church, commissioned by the city of Dresden, was created by George Bähr and realized between 1726 and 1743. The fact that Bähr was able to prevail with his visionary proposal of an elaborate dome construction was probably due not least to the absolutist need for self-portrayal and the preference of the Elector and Duke of Saxony, August the Strong, for St. Peter's Basilica in Rome and the Church of Santa Maria della Salute in Venice with its domes, but was also due to the requirement to build upwards in a very limited space. In order to be able to support the 12,000-ton dome in the end, it was made of Elbe sandstone instead of wood—an additional challenge for the master builder. As a result, the Evangelical Lutheran Church is probably the largest sandstone building in the world. However, sandstone was also its undoing, as it was not heat-resistant. After the bombing of Dresden on the night of February 14 to 15, 1945, the church, which had last been restored in 1938, burned down and collapsed on February 15. On its own ruins, it was faithfully rebuilt with the stones stored on the outskirts of the city, as well as newly processed ones and, after nearly ten years of construction, reopened in 2005.

FRAUENKIRCHE MIT NEUMARKT

Fig.1-7 Church of Our Lady, 1898

Dresden Cathedral (Hofkirche) : Spatially and temporally, the Catholic Dresden Cathedral [Fig.1-8] and the Protestant Church of Our Lady are far more connected than separated. Only 300 meters away from Church of Our Lady and only 10 years later in 1739, the construction of the Dresden Cathedral was started. It is considered one of the major works of the Dresden Baroque and was planned and built—by order of Frederick August II of Saxony, Elector of Saxony, King of Poland and Grand Duke of Lithuania (1696-1763)—by the Roman architect and master builder Gaetano Chiaveri (1689-1770). Today's Cathedral of the Diocese of Dresden-Meissen, which is under the patronage (patrocinium) of the Most Holy Trinity, was considerably destroyed no less than the other buildings in the city center by the bombing of February 13 to 15, 1945—not only the roof and the vault, but also exterior walls collapsed due to the massive use of demolition bombs.

Fig.1-8 Dresden Cathedral, 2011

Fig.1-9 Taschenberg Palace before WWII

Taschenberg Palace (Taschenbergpalais) : Built at the beginning of the 18th century in the "lush Dresden Baroque style" on a small hill, the Taschenberg Palace [Fig.1-9], as a representative city palace, was a gift from King August the Strong to his mistress. Destroyed during the air raids on Dresden, the building was a ruin until 1992. After its reconstruction (at a cost of over 120 million Euros) in 1995, it is used commercially as the luxurious 5-star Kempinski Hotel with over 200 rooms and suites.

Yenidze Tobacco Factory: Apparently, there were times in Dresden when a factory modeled on a mosque with a minaret not only did not cause any lasting offence, but was even considered acceptable and effective for advertising. On the one hand, the special architecture was due to the (municipal) requirement that factory buildings could only be erected in a residential area if they fit into its overall image, and on the other (entrepreneurial) hand, that it should serve a special advertising purpose. Against this background, the tobacco manufacturer Hugo Zietz decided at the beginning of the 20th century to build a factory building the exterior architecture of which would resemble a mosque (the industrial chimney a minaret) and bear the name of the region from which he obtained his tobacco. This building [Fjg.1-10], which was later often admired, was not spared, at least not initially, the fate that usually befalls all architecturally exceptional buildings: It initially met with fierce resistance. World War II also left considerable traces of destruction upon it.

Fig.1-10 Former Yenidze Tobacco Factory, 1907-1912

The Blockhouse (Blockhaus): It was built from 1732 to 1755, and was also destroyed in the war but was reconstructed from 1978 to 1980 in accordance with its original appearance [Fig.1-11].

The so-called **Summer or Garden Palace** (Sommer-oder Gartenpalais) : It was a pleasure palace [Fig.1-12] of the Saxon princely court built around 1680, dominating the Great Garden, Dresden's city park, and is considered an art-historically important starting point of the Dresden Baroque. It, too, was badly hit and vastly destroyed by the bombardment. In the meantime, its exterior architecture has been restored.

Fig.1-11 The Blockhouse

Fig.1-12 Summer or Garden Palace

Fig.1-13 Stairwell in the Old Country House

The Old Country House (Altes Landhaus): The building was built between 1770 and 1776, and destroyed down to the outer shell during World War II. After an extensive restoration, it serves as the city museum and city gallery [Fig.1-13].

Fig.1-14 Villa Weigang

The magnificent building, **Villa Weigang** was built in 1903 and, due to the immense cost, thereof, also known as the Million Villa [Fig.1-14], did not escape the fate of the bombing and was more or less severely affected by it. After its reconstruction, it was used for various purposes.

German Hygiene Museum: Founded in 1912 by the entrepreneur and philanthropist Karl August Lingner, the museum was dedicated to health education in the broadest sense. Its 1930 appearance, which owed much to the architect Wilhelm Kreis, reflected the Bauhaus style among other things. After its destruction in World War II, the building was rebuilt in GDR times and extensively renovated after the turn of the millennium. Today, the museum [Fig.1-15] attracts around 300,000 visitors every year, and in keeping with its original purpose, it provides various impulses for health education and health promotion, in addition, permanent and special exhibitions as well as events, not least for children. Inglorious was its refunctioning and racial ideological use during the time of National Socialism.

Fig.1-15 German Hygiene Museum, museum front entry way with Ball Thrower Statue, 2017

Garden City Hellerau: Just as the value of a coin is determined and increases by the fact that it is lacking in another, baroque ruling class architecture unfolds its fascinating effect especially when it stands out from an environment lacking in stimulation. Baroque architecture is the icing on the cake of usually monumental, pompous buildings of the political and economic elite at the expense of those who do not belong to it. Against the background of the connections herein indicated, it can only be surprising, according to a certain critical view of architecture, that the latter can also marvel at the buildings for which they bleed directly or indirectly, and do not adhere to the reverse hierarchy, which sees the architecturally successful single-family house or the "cheap apartment". Today we would say that the "tiny house" [Fig.1-16] is superior in adhering to both architectural ethics and practicality. It is precisely this type of "dwelling" that will be examined in conclusion. It is the neighborhood or the organic interweaving of production site and workers' settlement, whereby the initiator, the entrepreneur Karl Schmidt, was not only concerned with providing workers and their families with relatively high-quality housing close to the workplace, but also with integrating them into socially demanding production processes. Of course, this initiative and its structural realization were also appropriated by the National Socialists and ideologically functionalized. Today, the settlement, its cultural facilities, including the "Festival Theater", and workshops that still exist there connect to the original objectives.

Fig.1-16 Garden City Hellerau

Excursus: National Socialist Architecture

The fact that Dresden is seen primarily in connection with, not to say identified with, its opulent Baroque and its bridge art, and that the not infrequent architectural testimonies to its National Socialist past are often ignored, raises questions. One explanation, a not insignificant one in our context, might be that a National Socialist physiognomy of the city—which can easily be traced—could visibly diminish Dresden's victim role against the background of the bombing in February 1945. After all, the architecture marked by National Socialist buildings bears unmistakable witness to how strongly and rapidly National Socialism was able to take hold, also, and especially in Dresden, during the short, fateful period of its existence from 1933 to 1945.

Klotzsche Air War School: It was in northern district of Dresden, built in 1935 with, among other things, a two-story lecture hall building [Fig.1-17], and its background is significant. Here, from 1936 to 1945, fighter pilots of the German Air Force were trained, thus continuing a training practice that was expressly forbidden by the *Treaty of Versailles* in 1919 but had already begun during the Wiemar Republic—under strict secrecy. From 1924 to 1933, against the background of the *Treaty of Rapallo*, trainee pilots were trained on fighter aircraft at an air base in Russia—the annual training average was 240 trainee pilots. In the same year, 1935, when Hitler, disregarding the *Treaty of Versailles*, ordered the creation of an air force, the Dresden Air War School, in the typical style of "homeland security" (Heimatschutz) architecture, was built. Curiously, both the Air War School and the adjacent airfield were spared from the February bombing, which does not play an insignificant role in the ethical assessment of the bombing. This fact may underscore that the bombing was a pure act of terrorism or war crime in that it was obviously not specifically aimed at militarily relevant objects.

Fig.1-17 Klotzsche Air War School, entrance area

Among the few buildings constructed in Dresden during the National Socialist period of government was the **District Air Command** (Luftgaukommando): It was built between 1935 and 1938 [Fig.1-18], noted architectural parallels with the Hygiene Museum and served the Wehrmacht Air Force to monitor military and civil aviation. After the war, the building (reflecting the architecture of the German Air Force) was initially the seat of the state government. From 1959 to 1989, it was used by the National People's Army of the GDR. Today, parts of it serve as an administrative building for the German Armed Forces (Bundeswehr)—a vivid example of core congruities of political systems.

The fact that Dresden was one of the largest military bases of the Third Reich does not at all fit into the idea of a Dresden that is highly esteemed for its cultural achievements. It also does not fit into the image that the generally perceived Dresden was hit at the end of the war, and from a historical distance we may even say—following the military strategy—that it was bound to be hit. Whether and how "inevitable", however, is a matter of controversy. We will return to the questions further down. That the context of "He who sows the wind will reap the whirlwind" can also be applied to Dresden is already suggested by the unmistakable view of its short but—at least in its beginnings—intensive National Socialist building history. Dresden is not the National Socialist blameless victim that—to its own great surprise and viewed through the glasses of a brown (National Socialist) minority—was completely unjustified and unjustly hit by the devastating February bombing.

It is to Matthias Donath's credit that he has gone in search of traces with regard to National Socialist architecture. That he was able to do this in an impressive manner is certainly also the result of his ability to connect the characteristics of National Socialist architecture with local architectural peculiarities and also to appreciate the structural yields of the architectural mix as an overall social achievement. The fact that the neoclassical style with its angular construction, which was so highly regarded by Hitler, did not prevail in Dresden is certainly also due to the fact that respected architects—we leave aside the ethical side of this action for the moment—were able to serve the Third Reich and bring their preferences for certain architectural styles along with them and into the new building projects. With this context in mind, Donath noted that the widespread notion of a "fascist architecture" owed itself not to reality but to the ideal image of National Socialist propaganda. Thus, if we do not find National Socialist architecture in pure culture in Dresden, this does not mean that there was no National Socialist building activity. The opposite was the case.

Fig.1-18 District Air Command for the supervision of military and civil aviation, 1938

Fig.1-19 Planned District Forum in Dresden, ca. 1938

Although the Dresden's **District Forum** (Gauforum) was not realized, its conception [Fig.1-19] throws an impressive spotlight on the considerable dynamism of National Socialist building projects. On the other hand, the administrative building of the State Farmers' Union, the airport with the Air War School for officer training in 1935 and the District Air Command, which served to supervise military and civil aviation, were realized, as was the construction of 20,000 new apartments. It is worth mentioning that all these could be accomplished in the short period of six years. After the outbreak of the war, however, there were limits to all plans of monumental buildings on the one hand and social housing on the other.

Art

The first thing that catches the eye when looking at Dresden is its baroque architecture as a special feature of its outer shell. Behind this hides a considerable wealth of (further) art. It was partly saved from its destruction in the war, but to a large extent, it became its irreversible victim. Dresden and its architecture, Dresden and its art—the annual (continuously growing) number of visitors alone illustrates its uniqueness. Dresden itself is a cultural treasure and is home to countless cultural treasures. In the following, we can again only allow ourselves a brief, exemplary look at them.

Like any other city, Dresden likes to boast of its famous daughters and sons who reached fame, whether they were born there, grew up there, were active there in some form or another for a short or long period of time, or simply died there. Even if Dresden's list of celebrities is not overwhelmingly long, it does include one or two well-known names. We want to capture some of them in the following. The selection follows subjective criteria. Not mentioned celebrities do not deserve less appreciation.

Dresden can be particularly proud of one of its artists, the Italian veduta painter **Bernardo Bellotto** (1721/1722-1780), also and especially known in Germany and Poland as Canaletto. His special view of the city of Dresden [Fig.1-20]—he had similar views of Vienna, Turin and Warsaw—can be admired in numerous oil paintings in the Semper Art Gallery.

Fig.1-20 Bernardo Bellotto: *The Old Market as viewed from the Castle Lane*, 1751

Caspar David Friedrich (1774-1840): An inscription in honor of him sums up the attitude of the draftsman and painter of the German Romantic Period: "The painter should not merely paint what he sees before him, but also what he sees within himself. If he therefore sees nothing in himself, he should also refrain from painting what he sees in front of him." A native of the Greifswald in north, Friedrich is considered a pioneer of early German Romanticism and Modern Art (as opposed to Baroque and Classicism). Nature and religion, illness and death and their interpretations play a central role in the artist's works. Frederich, who moved to Dresden in 1798 and later held an extraordinary professorship there in 1824, came forward in his own works with his own experiences, feelings and reflections [Fig.1-21]. He was distanced from the later Realism in landscape painting.

Fig.1-21 Caspar David Friedrich: *Easter Morning* (*Ostermorgen*)

Fig.1-22 Adrian Ludwig Richter: *Civitella*

Adrian Ludwig Richter (1803-1884): Born and died in Dresden, and so with a true Dresden native, he is one of the most famous German painters and for good reason professor of landscape painting at the Academy of Arts in Dresden. Richter left behind not only more than 2,500 woodcuts and, in addition to etchings, drawings and book illustrations, a biographical writing. His pioneering landscape painting in the style of late Romanticism and Biedermeier was inspired not least by the river landscape of his homeland, the charm of the Elbe, and the beauty of the landscape around Dresden [Fig.1-22].

Otto Dix (1891-1969): The fact that reality also has other things in store and that these are captured and reproduced by artists through sometimes unadorned visual material is taught by the works of art created in Dresden by no less talented artists, especially in the 1920s and 1930s. Dix is one of them. Dresden may be particularly proud of him, proud in even two respects, as namely his artistic creation is impressive not only on the surface of expression and the merging of idea and message which underlies his skilled creativity, but also and especially because it reflects civic, political positioning in difficult times. Works by him are exhibited in the Museum of Modern Art, among other places, underscoring the worldwide recognition of the painter and graphic artist.

Two of his works should be highlighted here from his oeuvre. Their subject matter interests us in a special way in the context of our view of Dresden, which was still so badly affected at the end of World War II: his painting *Trenches* (*Schützengraben*) (1921-1923) and his triptych *The War* (*Der Krieg*) (completed in 1932). In both works, Dix dealt with the reality of war. In both, he introduced the midst of chaos and misery from the perspective of the participant observer. "The painter," said Dix, "is the eye of the world." In this sense, Dix looked at the reality of war and conveys the misery associated with it in all clarity. It should be noted that his view and corresponding mediation are based on his own painful experiences as a war volunteer in World War I.

That Dix not only had belonged to the circle of those accused of "degenerate" art by the Hitler regime because of these two works, but also lost his professorship in Dresden, is not surprising. The National Socialist critics were outraged by the pacifist and anarchist content of these works of art and saw in them contributions to the decomposition of the "defense morale" (Wehrkraft). In their eyes, the works were nothing more than an expression of degeneration and cultural decay. This discreditation of artists and their creative works was motivated primarily by theory of race and resulted in an exhibition called "Degenerate Art" to go on tour. Created in Dresden in 1933, it served as a "sample collection" for the subsequent Munich exhibition with the same title. As Christoph Zuschlag points out, the "Female Show" (Femeschau) was clearly directed against the expressionist, left-wing political art of the artists united in the Dresden group "The Bridge" (Die Brücke), the "Dresden Secession Group 1919" (Dresdner Sezession Gruppe 1919), and the "Association of Revolutionary Visual Artists of Germany" (Assoziation Revolutionärer Bildender Künstler Deutschlands), and was essentially the result of the personal confrontation of secondrate, conformist artists with the socially critical ones.

Erich Kästner (1899-1974): If there is a true-born Dresden "son" of Dresden (Dresden "Jung") among Dresden's celebrities, as a writer, journalist and poet, he deserves one of the first places among the great Dresden artists. If he became popular after World War II especially through his widely read and distributed children's books (*Emil and the Detectives*, *The Flying Classroom*, *The Double Lottie*), Kästner already made a name for himself in the Weimar Republic through his socially critical, especially anti-militaristic writings. His outspoken anti-National Socialist stance earned him, like many others, a book ban. He had to bear witness to the public burning of his own books in Dresden in 1933. He remained true to his pacifist line even after the end of World War II—from 1951 to 1962, he was even president of the West German P.E.N. Center (International Association of Poets, Playwrights, Editors, Essayists and Novelists)—taking a firm stand against the rearmament policy of Konrad Adenauer and his government. Today, schools bearing his name, streets and squares commemorate the honest and upright artist [Fig.1-23]. In 2000, on his 101st birthday, the Erich Kästner Museum was opened in his honor in Dresden, which features a novel museum concept and attracts guests from all over the world.

Fig.1-23 Erich Kästner Sculpture in front of the Kästner Café

Gret Palucca (1902-1993): While Kästner was born in Dresden and later died in Munich, conversely, one of Dresden's very great artists died in Dresden after being born in Munich. Palucca is the artist in question [Fig.1-24]. Anyone, who like her, that had made it onto a stamp of the series "Women of German History" (1998), must have achieved something special. Gret Palucca made a name for herself as a dancer and dance instructor by developing—at a critical distance from classical dance and ballet—a special form of expressive dance, with restrictions during the National Socialist era, and was a much sought-after and highly decorated dancer for many decades. For Palucca, dance was not primarily a standardized craft, but an expression of a spiritual process. Today, the Palucca University of Dance in Dresden commemorates the highly deserving representative of the "New Artistic Dance".

Mary Wigman (1886-1973): Before Gret Palucca, her teacher, Mary Wigman, who was born in Hanover and died in Berlin and the pioneer of expressive dance, had already made it onto a stamp of the German Federal Post Office. Her dance performances, her choreographic creations, and her dance pedagogy made her world famous. The fact that she was not prepared on principle to place dance under the dominance of music, and that she sometimes even danced without musical references, helped her to achieve a high level of recognition, especially in intellectual circles. In 1920, she opened her school for modern dance in Dresden.

Fig.1-24 Gret Palucca

Victor Klemperer (1881-1960): Only through the meticulously written diaries of the publicist, philologist and politician Victor Klemperer and, not least, through his investigations into the *Language of the Third Reich* (*Lingua Tertii Imperii*) are we granted a subjective-authentic view of Dresden before, during and after the war. In person, Klemperer is the condensation of different currents: The conversion from Judaism to Protestantism; dropping out of school, his apprenticeship, and later university, and in the end nevertheless remained ungraduated, receiving a Doctorate and obtaining a position as University lecturer in 1914; volunteering for military service in World War I in 1915; from 1920 to 1935, he held a professorship at the Technical University of Dresden; living abroad; the revocation of his professorship by the Dresden Gauleiter himself; being a victim of a bombing in February 1945, then fleeing and returning to Dresden all in the same year; resuming his professorship; assuming political responsibility in the GDR as a member of the People's Chamber (Volkskamme) from 1950 to 1958; writing a journalistic reappraisal of one of the most eventful periods of German history: German Empire, Weimar Republic, Third Reich, postwar period with division of Germany into West and East.

The following examples only hint at the fact that Dresden was a center of attraction for celebrities from the fields of literature, music and painting, and also a place of residence for some of them for a short or long period of time: **Friedrich Schiller** visited Dresden in 1785, **Wolfgang Amadeus Mozart** in 1789, and **Johann Wolfgang von Goethe** in 1790 at the invitation of Christian Gottfried Körner, a patron of the arts. Schiller's presence is marked today by a monument to Schiller and the so-called "Little Schiller House" (Schillerhäuschen). From 1814 to 1849, his participation in the Dresden May Revolution followed by an arrest warrant, **Wilhelm Richard Wagner** (1813-1883) not only lived in Dresden but also developed his musical obsession here. **Karl May** (1842-1912), one of the most widely read writers in Germany and the most translated German author, moved into a villa in

Radebeul near Dresden in 1896. At the end of a broad life's work, characterized by adventure literature, the author positioned himself conspicuously as a pacifist. Between 1917 and 1931, among others, the Austrian-born **Oskar Kokoschka** (1886-1980), painter and writer of Expressionism and Viennese Modernism, also stayed in Dresden, where he completed professorship at the Art Academy.

The list could easily be continued, including prominent figures from the world of art who were not only temporarily resident in Dresden or who were only peripherally anchored in Dresden. In particular, we should mention those artists who, in the 1920s and 1930s, under the names "New Objectivity" (Neue Sachlichkeit) and "Verism" (Verismus), attempted to describe reality from a rational, socially critical distance in a disillusioning, unembellished, precise and soberly meticulous manner—from the observer's perspective, so to speak—using the possibilities of art given to them without exaggeration, in such a way that even the masses would be outraged by the—factual, visible—conditions and would want to change them. In addition to Otto Dix, Curt Querner, Otto Griebel and Hans Grundig, among many others, should be mentioned here.

But it is not only in the visual arts that we encounter "New Objectivity", but also in architecture [Fig.1-25], which stands out from Expressionism through strikingly clear geometric building fronts, through cool, plain and unadorned forms, which is characterized by simplicity, practicality and objectivity (parallels to the Bauhaus style developed in Weimar cannot be denied). Despite all the criticism of National Socialism of the New Objectivity, its representatives and contents, its stylistic elements characterized by purism can even be traced in buildings that were actually committed to a National Socialist conception of art (example as Klotzsche airport building). In the past, the New Masters Art Gallery has done much to highlight New Objectivity through appropriate exhibitions as a significant contribution of the Dresden art scene to the

Fig.1-25 New Objectivity: People's Bathhouse, Sachsenbad

development of art in Germany and beyond.

It was not long ago that inglorious headlines in the world press were devoted to a robbery in Dresden. Thieves had mysteriously broken into the treasury of the **Green Vault** on November 25, 2019, and stolen crown jewels of immeasurable value from a display case in the Jewel Room. With the art heist and the headlines it caused, the historical significance of the permanent exhibition in Dresden and with it the Green Vault located in the Royal Palace once again entered the consciousness of art lovers—a positive effect.

Dresden rightfully enjoys a worldwide reputation for its collections and exhibits of national art in 15 museums spreading throughout the city (including the Old Masters Picture Gallery, the Green Vault, the Museum of Prints and Drawings, the Mathematical-Physical Salon, the Armory, the Museum of Ethnology, the Sculpture Collection and the Porcelain Collection). The **porcelain collection** exhibited in Zwinger, displaying porcelain not only from China and Japan, but also from the neighboring Meissen, is likely among the most highly valued of these. Against the background of the fact that—one may put it so casually, but just thereby aptly—August the Strong had taken a liking to the art of East Asian porcelain and built up an exorbitant collection [Fig.1-26], it is to be understood that in Meissen, according to the Chinese or also the Japanese models, an equally unique porcelain manufacturer with worldwide reputation was created.

Considering the abundance and fragility of the artworks (from paintings to porcelain) housed in Dresden before the wars (World War I and World War II) and during the war, the importance of Dresden as a center of art is not only explained, but what is also brought to our attention is how culturally far-reaching war can be with its potential for destruction. The fact that the art, admired in Dresden today, survived the war is due to the sensitivity of contemporaries who knew, even under adverse conditions, that art must also be protected.

Fig.1-26 Chinese porcelain from the Medici donation, 1590 [Jingdezhen, China, Jiajing Era (1522-1566), the Ming Dynasty (1368-1644)]

Location and Surroundings

Dresden would not be Dresden if it were reduced to its inner city and thereby to its (external) architecture. It includes, in addition to "Saxon Switzerland", the Elbe meadows, such as the Elbe castles [Fig.1-27], the villa districts and the Pillnitz Castle. In addition to the Old Town of Dresden and various other quarters, the nearer and wider surroundings of Dresden were also the target of the enemy military counterattack and were accordingly affected. In connection with the destruction of historically unique buildings, countless art treasures (especially interior furnishings and collections of paintings) were also destroyed. These cannot be discussed either in terms of their extent or in detail. We will stick to the buildings as an indicator of the degree of destruction, but we also want to keep in mind the location of Dresden on the Elbe and its nearer and wider surroundings.

Fig.1-27 Albrechtsburg Castle, Meissen

Landscape

How strongly landscape leaves an indelible impression on people is brought to our awareness through the countless works of those individuals among us who have a more sensitive disposition, especially the poets and thinkers, the writers, visual artists and musicians. Elaborations upon their appreciation of landscape with regard to the formation of various mentalities would easily deserve their own volumes. Whether I grow up near a river or in a mountain range, in the city or in the countryside, does not have an insignificant effect on my worldview. The two creation myths in the first book of the collected biblical writings (Genesis or Genesis 1) are vivid examples: one myth told against the background of water, the other shaped by its location on land. Both narrate creation against different backgrounds, but different only on the narrative surface in that both seek to express at their core that the world is a created one. Contrary to what the frequently used depiction of a river as a "natural border" suggests, it is to be argued here that it is precisely at a river—no matter how wide it may be—that the mentalities and the natural sense of community and connection between the people settling along it not only coincide to a considerable degree but are naturally congruent. Where this is not the case, supposed contrasts are intentional and ideologically generated out of the interests of domination, landscape shapes. Dresden, the city on the Elbe, is a vivid example. The Elbe does not divide Dresden and the surrounding landscape into two parts but connects them into a whole [Fig.1-28].

Fig.1-28 Dresden's location on the Elbe River

Its location on a river that rises in the Giant Mountains (Riesengebirge) in the Czech Republic near the border with Poland, and connects it with the North Sea, imprints the cityscape with a mixture of tranquility and cosmopolitanism. The fact that the sublimity and fragility, pride and misery of a city can lie close together in its connection with a river was deeply engraved in Dresden's recent history. When in 2002, the Elbe, among the 100 largest rivers in the world, once again burst its banks, flooding the city on a hitherto unknown scale, foreseen by no one and leaving behind damage amounting to a billion Euros [Fig.1-29]. Although flooding is a regular occurrence in Dresden, and there have been previous exceptional floods (such as in 1845 and 1890, and then in 2006 and 2013), this one left the population of Dresden with a lasting shock. But it is not only in Dresden that the effects of the flood have not been forgotten to this day. Once again, the unexpected had occurred. Here, too, Dresden weighed itself in relative safety in its dealings with nature and did not want to face the extreme prematurely. It was only afterwards that it took the preventive measures—with a considerable monetary investment—that it could have taken earlier if it had had some imagination. Of course, outsiders in particular always know better in retrospect, and it is easy to pass judgment from a retrospective perspective.

The demonstration of splendor and power in an ensemble of representative buildings combined with the location on the river has inspired many artists. The most famous among them is, undoubtedly, Bernardo Bellotto. He captured the Dresden of his time in engaging paintings not least for posterity. His originals can be admired in the Old Masters Picture Gallery. Bellotto allows us a heartfelt view of the city from two different directions: from the right bank of the Elbe above and below the Augustus Bridge (Augustusbrücke) [Fig.1-30].

Fig.1-29 Elbe-flooding in 2002, flooded central train station (left) and its normality (right)

Not by Bernardo Bellotto and a good 150 years later (between 1890 and 1905), another impressive picture was probably created. It presents a view from the War Ministry on the stately Augustus Bridge and the striking urban backdrop, to the left of it Church of Our Lady and to the right the Dresden Cathedral. The Augustus Bridge is known to be the largest bridge built in the German High Middle Ages and one of the largest medieval transport structures in Europe.

Fig.1-30 Bernardo Bellotto: *View of Dresden from the right bank of the Elbe below the Augustus Bridge*, 1748, the Old Masters Picture Gallery

Just as the architectural or artistic flair of Dresden gives visitors and locals alike a Mediterranean feeling of life, so—one might think—part of Dresden's hinterland with its rugged rocky landscape allows one to catch a glimpse of Switzerland. With reference to its province Saxony, this stretch of land is therefore also called "Saxon Switzerland" [Fig.1-31].

Saxon Switzerland(on the Czech side, referred to as Bohemian Switzerland), which rises southeast of Dresden, is a part of the Elbe Sandstone Mountains extending on both sides of the Elbe. Characteristics are its geologically highly interesting table mountains and bizarre rock formations, and its highest elevation being the Great Zschirnstein with about 560 m. Comparisons with American national parks or the world-famous limestone hills characteristic for Guilin and decorating the walls of many Chinese restaurants are imposing.

The tranquility and wilderness of the landscape have influenced not only composers Carl Maria von Weber and Richard Wagner, but also painters such as Caspar David Friedrich and Adrian Ludwig Richter. More than 1,000 climbing peaks invite to be climbed. The type of climbing is strictly regulated according to aspects of sustainability, and only climbers are allowed to spend the night under the distinctive rock outcrops (the so-called "Boofen") in Saxon Switzerland, a national park since 1990. This is known in jargon as "boofen", which perhaps could be translated into English as "boofing", and which is in no way connected to the English use of the word of boofing.

Fig.1-31 Saxon Switzerland

Castles and Palaces

Whoever looks at castles and palaces usually cannot escape their charisma and is often unaware that in this case she or he is only "considering" one side of the story: the stately one. That another view, the view of the dwellings of the lesser folk, in fact presents us with a completely different form of architecture, which is not always easy to realize. Rulership, through shape and mass, is much more easily conserved over time. Just as the objects of social history associated to the care of the family, to food and work, are far less easy to locate and represent in comparison with those derived from monumental buildings (stones) and war (weapons), so the periphery of the architectural testimonies of domination and power usually remain hidden from viewers. Notwithstanding this problem, but knowing it, a selection of dominion architectural highlights will be taken up here in the sense of a reflection of the productive power of Dresden's hinterland. It is especially the connection of Dresden's river landscape with the ensemble of Elbe castles that makes up a special bouquet of sights.

When viewing Dresden, one cannot help but see its scenic and architectural surroundings and in particular its impressive Elbe castles. With its captivating grounds and architecture, the baroque **Residential Palace of Pillnitz** (construction began in 1721 under the direction of Matthäus Daniel Pöppelmann) stands out in a very special way. The palace with its considerable estate is located on the right bank of the Elbe [Fig.1-32], about 15 km southeast of Dresden. In addition to the usual routes (car and public transport), it can also be reached by water on one of the usual tourist boats, an original paddle steamer, or even a salon ship along the Elbe.

Asian visitors, especially those from China, will not miss the opportunity to visit the **Chinese Pavilion** (built in 1804) situated on a tranquil pond [Fig.1-33], and linger under the old trees surrounding the replica of East Asian pavilions.

Another pearl among the sights in Dresden's vicinage is the baroque **Moritzburg Moated Castle** [Fig.1-34], located 20 km north of Dresden. It served as a hunting residence for the Saxon electors. In particular, Elector Augustus the Strong spared no investment to give the castle the royal splendor that was so important to him personally.

Even if it is not located in the immediate vicinity of Dresden, an exemplary collection of castles and fortresses is one that should not be missing: **Königstein Fortress** [Fig.1-35], located 40 km southeast of Dresden, on a high plateau (about 250 m above the Elbe River). With its almost 2-km-long rampart and its walls, some of which are almost 50 m high, it is one of the largest castle fortresses in Europe. Its 150 m deep well is also a superlative. During its 800-year history, marked by countless alterations, it served not only as a fortress, but also as a hunting lodge and pleasure palace, as a monastery and state prison, as a prisoner-of-war camp and military hospital, as a repository for state reserves and important archival holdings including works of art (this also during World War II), as a bunker, and finally, as an open-air museum of military history. Over a period of 50 years from 1955 to 2005, the fortress attracted 25,000,000 visitors, and alone in 2018 about half a million people visited the castle.

Fig.1-32 The Residential Palace of Pillnitz

Fig.1-33 Chinese Pavillion in the park of Pillnitz Castle

Fig.1-34 Moritzburg Moated Castle

Fig.1-35 Königstein Fortress

Society

Between the end of World War I and the beginning of the World War II, there are no more than a good two decades between 1918 and 1939—a time of dense social processes and revolutionary political and economic developments. How people lived in Dresden at that time can only be roughly sketched and selectively described in the following. A look at this period may be helpful in order to better understand what they had experienced, especially at the end of World War II, and how this potentially affected them. Dresden, as it turns out, is not only about baroque architecture and art.

Prewar Era

Since Dresden was one of the largest garrison cities during World War I and was an armaments center, the disarmament requirements of the victorious powers at the end of World War I hit the city particularly hard. The conversion of the economy to a peacetime economy was difficult and protracted. Holger Starke describes the economic situation, which was not only associated with high unemployment, as devastating at the time. On the other hand, Dresden experienced not only rapid industrial development, but also considerable progress in transportation, including aviation. Great personal hardship resulted from the burden of high reparation payments, the world economic crisis and the devaluation of money. With the "Annual Shows of German Labor", the city tried to counteract this in a targeted

Fig.1-36 Dresdeners enjoying their weekend at the Klotzsche Bath

manner and to stimulate economic development.

On the one hand, Dresden's residents were heavily burdened by the search for work and securing their subsistence by earning a regular living; on the other hand, however, they also sought pleasure in their leisure time: in particular, they discovered cinema for themselves and photography, they played sports in various clubs (segmented according to worldview and social status), sang and hiked, rode bicycles, swam [Fig.1-36] and rowed, spent their time in their allotment gardens, and sometimes cultivated a nudist body cult.

Based on photo albums made available to the author, Jürgen Richter has lovingly illustrated life in Dresden in the 1920s in a humorous way, considering every conceivable aspect of life, as the titles and subtitles of his volume suggest in the following few examples: "Dresden roles into action. In 1921, 22 locations were incorporated." "The skirt makes the difference. Not only in private schools are girls and boys separate." "Only billionaires get beer. Inflation is the legacy of World War I." "Nudist bathing with view of the castle. When the Elbe still enticed people to swim in her waters." "Monotonous salt. Dresden architects set some striking signs." "Wire from the town hall to the sky. In 1923, a radio program is received for the first time."

Anyone wishing to gain information about everyday life in Dresden in the 1920s would be well advised to take a look at the contemporary color illustrated magazines *Eagle Owl* (*Uhu*), *The Cross-Section* (*Der Querschnitt*) and *The Magazine* (*Das Magazin*). Magazines of this kind are a treasure trove in the search for impressions of life together between the wars. A major digitization project is now bringing the magazines' contents to an interested public by providing user-friendly Internet access and eliminating the need for complicated trips to the archives.

Just how great the interest in the 1920s and 1930s is, is underscored by the plethora of exhibitions that increasingly focus on precisely these periods under different headings. To pick just one example: the 2019 exhibition at the city museum of Dresden entitled "Dresden Modernism 1919 to 1933. New Ideas for the City, Architecture and People". It is not only intended, as the exhibition catalog states, to show the dynamics of a city in terms of building history, i.e. its innovative construction measures in the area of public buildings as well as private ones. It is also intended to present changing ideals of the body, high-rise fantasies, and ambitious museum projects, and to introduce visitors to the "exciting mixture" of democratic impulses, technological euphoria, and the flair typical of those years. In the process, the combination of value conservatism and open-mindedness that was characteristic of Dresden at the time is also expressed.

The 1920s were also marked by the fact that women were allowed to vote from the end of 1918 and had to replace men's labor in many areas—many had not returned from World War I. Women began to smoke in public. Thus, the 1920s were also marked by the emergence of a new image of women. In art, sexuality and violence were thematized against the background of war-related traumatization.

Strictly speaking, the Roaring Twenties actually lasted only five years, from 1924 to 1929. Yet even during this period, splendor and misery were close together. An attempted coup and a Ruhr uprising in 1920 and hyperinflation in 1923. A brief economic upswing starting in 1924 was followed by the world economic crisis in 1929, resulting in the German banking crisis in 1931. In Germany, the economic boom lasted only from 1926 to 1928, and internal social divisions quickly came to a dangerous head. Despite all attempts at stabilization, the young parliamentary system was unable to prevent National Socialism from seizing power. In 1933, only 15 years after the end of World War I, Adolf Hitler proclaimed the so-called "Thousand-Year Reich". It was only 6 years later that Hitler and his claqueurs plunged Germany and the world into a war that far surpassed the inconceivable horrors of World War I. Over 60 million people alone lost their lives in it. Sociopolitical developments in Dresden can also be seen and understood in the larger economic and political context between the two World Wars.

The extent and intensity of construction activities were limited by the conditions of the postwar period, and later by the concentration of economic resources on the requirements of World War II. The priority after World War I was the construction of housing and housing estates, which had come to a standstill during the war. While there was hardly any need for new industrial buildings due to the retrofitting of existing ones, the reason for which no significant development in the field of industrial architecture can be traced, individual urban high-rise buildings did attract attention. Dresden's connection to the imperial motorway was significant in terms of transportation policy. Larger building projects planned after Hitler's seizure of power in many cases did not get beyond the planning stage. In terms of monument preservation, restoration work on Zwinger and Church of Our Lady, as well as measures in the area of riverbank design, are particularly noteworthy.

As a result of the world economic crisis that began in 1929, the educational system with its elementary and secondary schools in Dresden, which was progressive in itself, had to accept considerable cuts. Prior to that, the school system in Dresden had certainly been a model, such as reduction of the number of students per class, abolition of all forms of corporal punishment of pupils by teachers, establishment of parents' councils, academic training of teachers, promotion of reforming pedagogical experiments, etc. Soon after the end of the World War I, Technical University of Dresden, which was developing considerably in many areas, rapidly came under the influence of brown ideology, or in other words, the ideology of national socialism.

The health care system, which had been able to develop a special profile in Dresden not only by investing in the construction and maintenance of clinics, but also with openings for naturopathy and the establishment of a sanatorium, as well as measures in the field of hygiene in particular and the international establishment of the so-called Hygiene Museum, also suffered severe cuts as a result of the world economic crisis.

Dresden was also a hub of culture in the "Roaring Twenties", of course, not for everyone, "a hotspot for the artistic avantgarde of Europe". "In the middle of the decade" according to a catalog published by the Dresden State Art Collections, "the art of Soviet Russian Constructivism, the Dutch The Style (De Stijl) movement, and the Bauhaus in particular caused a stir in tradition-saturated Florence on the Elbe." Alongside Expressionism, the art movement of New Objectivity established itself, i.e. the attempt to "see things completely naked, clearly—almost without art" in the eyes of Otto Dix. Dresden art galleries and exhibitions enjoyed an international reputation. However, the National Socialist exhibition "Degenerate Art" in 1933 put an end to the dynamism of the Dresden art scene as abruptly as it did brutally. From 1933, the pacifist, and revolutionary literary awakenings that had already begun during the war were also abruptly halted by the National Socialists. Well-known literary figures were forced to conform, fell silent or went into exile. The dilemma in which the literati found themselves was aptly expressed by Kurt Tucholsky in a letter to Walter Hasenclever in 1934: The answer to the question of what one wanted to live on now under the pressure of dictatorial dictates could not be to "eat dirt". Even the internationally renowned and expressive stage dance, strongly developed by the Dresden dance schools around Mary Wigman and Gret Palucca, could not escape its fate. Both schools, far from the philosophy on which they were based, were converted into purely training schools. As far as music was concerned, Dresden was also able to keep up internationally with its State Opera, State Orchestra and State Ballet, as well as orchestral culture, church and choral music. But the Nazi Party also brought about its downfall, not least through the deportation of highly talented Jewish musicians and their forced emigration. It is not surprising that the experimental theater and colorful stage styles also fell victim to National Socialist dictates.

The spirit of optimism after World War I, which was characterized by housing and road construction as well as welfare, was severely dampened in Dresden with the onset of the Great Depression, especially because its economy was overly dependent on exports and, in addition to reparation burdens, liabilities related to municipal bonds, bankruptcies and an explosion in the number of unemployed, which led to massive shifts in spending. For example, the number of unemployed rose from 30,000 in 1929 to 47,000 in 1930, to 70,000 in 1931 and 93,000 in 1933, and the number of citizens in need of support rose from 27,000 to 76,000 in the same period. Even if the Nazi Party's popularity in Dresden was lower than the Reich average, National Socialism was able to assert itself against opposition forces in Dresden as well, ultimately by sheer force. Public life was brought into line at all levels.

National Socialism

Right at the beginning of his historical travel guide through the Dresden of the Hitler dictatorship from 1933 to 1945, Hartmut Ellrich dispels any doubt that Dresden has a clear National Socialist past, and—one may conclude from this, of course without any cynicism—in this respect, in the end, also has itself to blame for the adequate consequences of such a liaison. The reference to the experience that "He who sows the wind will reap the whirlwind" is not intended to relativize the suffering that Dresden had to endure by interpreting the February bombing as a just punishment for the indescribable injustice that emanated from Nazi Germany and which cost millions their lives. Nevertheless, a connection may be made and marked as such. In this sense, Ellrich positions himself as succinctly as he does clearly in the first section of his guidebook when he writes: "Even before the National Socialists 'seized power' on January 30, 1933, Dresden was a stronghold of the Nazi Party."

Because the mayor at the time resisted the takeover, he was removed from office in March 1933. Dresden became the capital of Saxony. The new National Socialist mayor simultaneously claimed the office of Minister President of Saxony, thus endowing himself with a hitherto unprecedented amount of power. That same month, "one of the first book burnings of the Third Reich" took place in Dresden [Fig.1-37]. "Numerous artists and scientists ... were chased out of the city. During the 'Night of Broken Glass' (Reichskristallnacht), Semper's Synagogue also went up in flames. The approximately 5,000 Jewish Dresdeners were expelled or deported to concentration camps. Dresden was one of seven 'redesign cities'. The banks of the Elbe were transformed into a parade ground, and the plan was to create a large district forum (Gauforum)."

Fig.1-37 On March 8, 1933, SA-Men, under the protection of police, burnt documents and books from the building that had been stormed which housed the Dresden People's Newspaper (Volkszeitung) and Kaden Publishers at Wettiner Square.

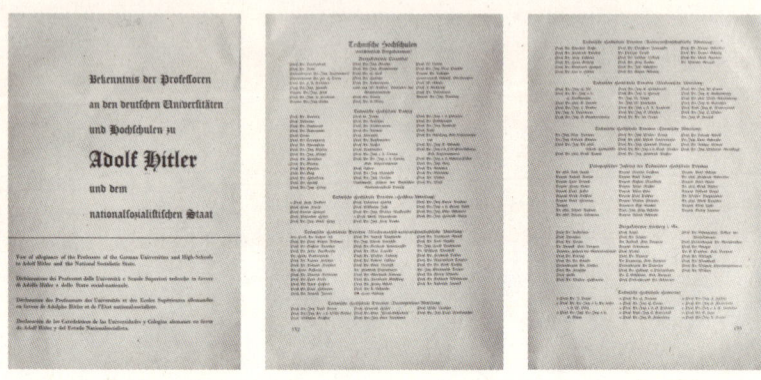

Fig.1-38 Excerpt from the *Confession of Professors at German Universities and Colleges to Adolf Hitler and the National Socialist State*, 1933

Last but not least, a part of the academic community (albeit a small one) paid tribute to the National Socialist regime and demonstratively declared their support—in public and by name—for Adolf Hitler [Fig.1-38]. On the eve of 11, November. 1933, they "legalizing" the withdrawal from the League of Nations that had been decided in a "referendum" on October 14 of the same year. Among them was also one of the great thinkers of the 20th century, Martin Heidegger, at that time head of the University of Freiburg. It requires only moderately great imagination to explain the connections: A part of the signatories, usually including professors, but also lecturers and teaching assistants, even students, might indeed have identified more or less with the National Socialist program in theory and practice, notwithstanding the encroachment of the Nazi Party within the framework of the political affairs of the Nazi Party by Adolf Hitler's power of command in all matters, on the freedom of research and teaching through ideological guidelines, removal of Jewish scholars from the teaching staff, or the presence of the Nazi Party at the universities. Another part of the signatories probably promised themselves—even under the condition that consent was not explicitly required—professional security or career advancement within the framework of National Socialist guidelines. The latter signed under the dictates of existential fears or the expectation of favoritism. Concessions in professional contexts in the interest of securing one's livelihood and, thus, of becoming a professional civil servant, were among the strongest and most reliable pillars of the acquisition and exercise of power. In this sense, many also joined the Nazi Party and were not always only in their own private interest. Frequently, they decided to become a member of the party in order to thereby better attain most honorable goals more easily if at all. They were often "more pontifical than the pope" and by their behavior even elevated the system, of which they were actually and conditionally critical. What historical research has meanwhile revealed in these cases is that the servility practiced by the members was often neither necessary nor explicitly demanded in this form. It was not infrequently an unnecessary excess, although in the aggregate a highly welcome one by the regime. That there were also other, even moderate ways of coexistence with the unjust regime, up to and including open, constructive opposition, is eloquently demonstrated by the other part of the Dresden professoriate. They did not sign the declaration—regardless of the conceivable consequences, for example the Faculty of Theology of the University of Marburg.

If many residents of Dresden certainly did not agree with these developments, which are only hinted at here, and at least those who did could not be held liable for the consequences for this reason alone, it may, nevertheless, be stated that these developments were able to take hold without the appropriate resistance. Therefore, those who did not inwardly agree with them had not positioned themselves sufficiently against them. This has consequences for postwar Dresden, where right-wing forces are once again at work, blatantly advocating a National Socialist policy, while others oppose it under the motto "Stop the beginnings" (Wehret den Anfängen) and stand up and campaign for a Dresden open to the world. There is no guarantee that developments cannot repeat themselves. Nationalism in conjunction with Populism will continue to be a "perennial issue" in the future. In the case of Dresden, this is all the more incomprehensible because the connection between doing and being done is particularly tangible here. The universally lamented bombing can be seen together without reservation with the diabolical actions of the National Socialist regime of injustice. The fact that it was able to come into being was due in no small part to Dresden's role as a National Socialist hotbed. It is no less true for Dresden than for Lubeck, Thomas Mann's father city, for example: That, as Mann is urged to state in view of the destruction of the old city by the British attacks, "there is nothing to be said against the doctrine that everything must be paid for", here with the explicit mention of Coventry.

As a reminder, as early as 1923, the then prime minister of Saxony felt he had to warn of a civil war in view of the gathering of fascist groups. In 1930, seven years later, the Nazi Party scored its party's first major electoral success in Saxony, of all places. With a clear commitment to the working class and anti-communist agitation, the National Socialist political strategy worked. Saxony became "brown" with meteoric speed. The fact that only a few years later it had to atone with terrible consequences for the loss of reality and megalomania expressed in the idea of a Thousand-Year Third Reich is not surprising, of course—and this is meant purely analytically. In the context of the question regarding the ethical evaluation of the bombardment, the reasons for it and the associated consequences, will be dealt with below.

2

Chapter 2

Dresden in World War II

Even though the chapter "Dresden before World War II" may have a travel-guide-like feeling in individual sections, it is not intended to and cannot even begin to provide what every travel guide about Dresden available on the market provides in terms of information about one of the most historically and culturally rich cities on our globe. This, in turn, may not exclude that one or the other reference might inspire one to travel to Dresden to obtain their own impression onsite.

The actual purpose of the subjectively exemplary excursion into the history and culture of Dresden is to present a world that is characterized by a special splendor and exudes its very own charm, and which, precisely against this background, must inevitably experience itself particularly hard hit by the force of war-typical destructiveness and fragility.

War, as was also to be shown in this context, always has a prior history. A war does not fall into one's lap, a war does not simply break out. Wars become impending, and wars drag on. On the eve of the World War I, many were looking forward to it as a blitzkrieg that, according to their ideas, could be easily won and quickly ended with the expectation of being back home by Christmas. In the end, the fourth Christmas, and it almost became a fifth Christmas, over which the war dragged on. As a rule, the reality of war catches up bitterly with war volunteers [Fig. 2-1]. They had imagined the whole thing differently. That it would end up costing the lives of an estimated 17 million people was certainly something that not only they, but most others as well, had not considered.

Fig.2-1 Bernhard Heisig: *The War Volunteer* (*Der Kriegsfreiwillige*)

War is hideous, war is inhuman, war is barbaric. This can easily be demonstrated by marking its place and time in the large context of before and after. Also, and especially in the case of Dresden, it can be shown that war is not the normal case. Instead, it is the terrible break in a story which for long and longest stretches of time is free of war and that has momentarily slipped out of the hands of the people responsible for it, either through carelessness or overconfidence. The environment in which war takes place—also and especially in Dresden—allows the grimace of its horror to emerge in a special way. Embedded in a fascinating landscape of prosperity, art and culture—this was only to be hinted at in the preceding chapter—the absurdity of the phenomenon imposes itself as a summed-up judgment.

The Context of War

Dresden's fate must also be placed in the reality of war itself, which is only hinted at here, in this inconceivable darkness of our human existence, and World War II in particular, and its active and passive participation on the one hand. Inevitably connected with this, its suffering from the war, on the other hand, must be seen and judged. The bombing of Dresden can only be rightly understood as one piece of the war puzzle, which is made up of an infinite number of pieces. In this puzzle, it played a significant role towards the end of the war, but against all appearances it did not play a central role, let alone a leading one.

Air Warfare—War from Above

Looking at *the Bomber's Baedeker* [Fig.2-2], the macabre target list of the British Royal Air Force, Dresden's turn for being bombed was comparatively late. In the end, on April 14, 1945, Potsdam, located southwest of Berlin, was hit—and even this only, according to Sven Felix Kellerhoff, because it had not yet fallen and the British simply "could" destroy it. The first list, drawn up in 1943, listed 392 German cities with more than 15,000 inhabitants as targets in the air warfare and, moreover, all targets within these cities that were relevant to raw materials, infrastructure or culture. A second list of *the Bomber's Baedeker*, compiled in 1944, shows that even all war-relevant cities with less than 1,000 inhabitants were potential bombing targets. The cities were categorized according to certain criteria of their war relevance, ranging from the lowest category 3 to the highest 1, which was topped by the special category 1+. Remarkably, there was no category 1+ target in Dresden, and the five category 1 targets were all spared in the February bombing, which underlines that the real strategy of the British Royal Air Force was aimed at the war morale of the population. The military sought to overcome this not by targeting military objects, but by bombing city centers and residential neighborhoods. The main aim was to weaken the war morale of industrial workers.

The fact that the name Baedeker was chosen or had to be used for the list is due to the well-known travel guides of the Baedeker Publishing House. Just as individual cities, historical buildings or cultural centers are singled out and described as relevant for a visit, the bombardments are also based on a selection of cities. In them, the bombing was intended to disrupt public life as sensitively as possible, for example as a reaction to the bombing of Lubeck and Rostock.

Baedeker raids were initially defined as the bombing of militarily insignificant but historically significant cities in England by the German Air Force in 1942. These were the militarily insignificant and therefore undefended cities of Exeter, Bath, Norwich, York and Canterbury. Other so-called Baedeker raids took place primarily in eastern England. The term "Baedeker Blitz", which was used by the British as well, was not unskilled in propaganda because it was so catchy and was used as a basis for the blanket bombardment of Germany by the Allies, especially the British and American air forces.

Fig.2-2 *The Bomber's Baedeker*

Although the importance of air warfare was already assessed in Great Britain at the turn of the century as a new and revolutionizing warfare and was underscored above all by a publication of the Italian Giulio Douhet in 1921, in which he already named the "will of the people" as the goal of the air warfare, the British government still expressly forbade the Bomber Command immediately after the beginning of the war to choose targets that would lead to high casualties among the civilian population. Two assumptions played a not insignificant role in this: that the bombing of decidedly military targets would minimize the heinous wars of position fought in World War I, while bombings that would indiscriminately hit the civilian population would cause horrendous casualties among them. Step by step, however, the British government not only abandoned its scruples about bombing the civilian population, but increasingly incorporated it into its overall strategy. Significant contributions to this included: The bombing of London in World War I by Zeppelins in 1915 and heavy bombers in 1917 with no apparent military benefit; experience in suppressing colonial uprisings by indiscriminately targeting combatants and civilians from the air, first done in 1911 by a bomb dropped by Italian pilot Giulio Gavotti; the bombing of Guernica in the Spanish Civil War by the German Condor Legion in 1937, which was also militarily meaningless; the bombing of Wieluń in Poland in 1939 by the German Luftwaffe, again without military benefit but with high civilian casualties; the bombing of Warsaw in 1939 and many other cities, not least Coventry in 1940, in which the civilian population with its centers of life— city centers, its infrastructural lifelines—traffic and its places of life—homes and workplaces were, by way of argument but not factually, always targeted, and military objects played a central role. Although the attacks were primarily aimed at breaking the population's will to war, they were also to a large extent purely retaliatory strikes. For example, as early as 1940, the British Royal Air Force responded to the bombing of Coventry with an area bombing campaign in Hamburg with the primary goal of hitting working-class neighborhoods and burning down the city center.

From the point of view of military strategy, the air war became more and more convincing and took its place in the overall strategy of the warring parties as decisive for the war. With regard to the advance of the Soviet Army in the context of the Allied liberation of Germany from the Hitler regime and a forcible end to World War II, it may certainly be stated that this would not have been possible in the known manner if the German Wehrmacht had not been disproportionately tied down and weakened on the Western Front by the air warfare of the other Allies. Whether the capture and occupation of Germany would have been possible on the basis of positional warfare alone is probably a purely theoretical question that can hardly be answered. Nevertheless, without wanting to misuse the victims of the Dresden bombardments in a numbers game, it may be asked in this context and against the background of the original work towards a warfare including proportional bombardments, purely theoretically, how high the casualties in and around Dresden could possibly have been in the context of a war of position and mere deployment of ground troops. For there could hardly have been any doubt in February 1945 that Dresden would also "fall" at some point and would have to surrender to the advancing Red Army. However, the comparison of air warfare and positional warfare also makes it clear that the victims in air warfare are primarily civilians, while in positional warfare, in the use of ground troops and man-to-man combat, it is primarily the warring soldiers themselves. Even if the decision for an air war instead of a war of position—and thus also the separation of front and rear—is based on the military strategic idea of shortening the war as a whole by prioritizing bombardments, the decision is in end made to prefer civilian casualties to military ones. To this day, the great powers increasingly shy away from using their own soldiers on the ground and in man-to-man constellations. This is not the case with anonymized bombing. Due to the high distance between pilot and victim, this not only reduces the inhibition towards killing, but also minimizes the danger for the pilot of becoming a victim himself. Those who suffer from this development—example Aleppo—are the civilians living in the war zone. They are the location-bound hostages in this kind of war.

Dresden was also part of an air warfare and can ultimately only be understood in this context. Therefore, here are a few more figures: While between 1939 and 1942 bombs amounting to about 90,000 tons were dropped over Germany, between 1943 and 1945 the figure was close to 1.5 million tons. To this day, bombs whose fuses had not been triggered can still be found during evacuation work, including in Dresden. While the British Royal Air Force lost 22,000 planes and 80,000 soldiers in the air warfare with Germany and the American 18,000 planes with also nearly 80,000 soldiers, Germany lost 57,000 fighters and bombers. Overall, the expectations that military leaders associated with a war from the air were met only to a limited extent. Adverse weather conditions and limitations in technical areas created restrictions that affected both the targeting accuracy of the attacks and the central goal of demoralizing the population.

Europe's Cities—Terror from the Air

The February bombing, which is the focus of our consideration here, is to be understood not only in the large context of the area bombings that Germany had to endure for reasons of military strategy, but also for reasons of retaliation and revenge, as a result of and even above all in the large context of what Germany brought to most European countries in terms of death and immeasurable suffering through its policy of aggression evoked by World War II. In order to merely hint at the scope of the impact, we focus our view on the air warfare on a few selected examples.

Actually, according to Wolfram von Richthofen as field marshal of the Condor Legion, the "complete eradication of Warsaw" was already envisaged in 1939. Then, on September 1, without risking any casualties, he was able to repeat with 87 fighter-bombers the work he had already tested in Guernica. Between 04:35 and 14:00, he razed 70% of the sleepy town of Wieluń [Fig.2-3] to the ground. Of the 16,000 inhabitants, 1,200 lost their lives. World War II began with a war crime.

These were followed in 1940 by Freiburg, a few days later Rotterdam on May 14, 1940 with the destruction of the entire old city, London from September 1, 1940 to May 16, 1941, Coventry from November 14 to 15, 1940, finally Belgrade from April 6 to 7, 1941, Moscow from July 22 to December 6, 1941, Leningrad from September 8, 1941 to January 27, 1944.

The picture that emerges from enumerations of this kind is to be filled with references to, for example, targeted bombardments of the population by on-board weapons of dive bombers up to the war crimes committed by members of the army, i.e. the ground troops. We think here, representative of many others, of Lidice [Fig.2-4], a small village near Prague, whose 172 male inhabitants (older than 15 years) were shot as an act of revenge on June 10, 1942. Of the 195 women deposited in the Ravensbrück concentration camp, 52 were

Fig.2-3 Wieluń, September 1, 1939

Fig.2-4 Shooting of the male population of Lidice

murdered there. In addition, other men were shot and pregnant women were also taken to the concentration camp after giving birth. The village was razed to the ground by the occupying forces not by area bombardment but by the war-criminal actions of ground troops.

To discuss and evaluate ethically the air raid on Dresden without taking at least a brief, selective look at the work of destruction carried out by Hitler's Germany, here in particular in the context of the area bombardments carried out by the German Luftwaffe, would not only be simply unfair. It would also skew an essential aspect of the evaluation perspective. The bombardment of Dresden cannot be judged ethically without seeing it in the broad spectrum of the unjust actions of fascist Germany, which contradict every ethos. To quote Christian Bangel again, "One cannot commemorate the victims of Dresden without naming the Lebensraum and racial ideology of the Nazis and mourning the many people, especially the Jews, who had been murdered by them by then, without remembering the many other cities in Europe that were destroyed by the Germans". As must be repeated here, "The horror of the Dresden bombing nights, has its origin in Germany". What is meant by this is that the whole incomprehensible misery, which in six indescribable years of war covered not only Europe, but directly or indirectly the whole world, and is therefore also called World War, was caused by Hitler's Germany. This, in turn, does not mean that only one person was responsible for it, but this person and all those who actively or passively supported and assisted him were as well. Seen in this way, injustice is not based on the actions of one particular person, but ultimately on the approval by countless claqueurs and on the system of fatal (supposedly) existential dependencies.

No war begins on a specific day X. Every war has a context and a history. In this respect, the timing of its beginning is a function of a diplomatic distancing, a de facto attack, an official declaration of war, or the like. For example, the assumption that World War II began with the invasion of Poland by soldiers of the German Wehrmacht on September 1, 1939, hides its prehistory, which can include the War of Resistance against Japan from September 18, 1931 to September 2, 1945. A massacre of the population of Nanjing (the capital of Republic of China at the time) carried out during World War II by Japanese invaders [Fig.2-5]—and thus allies of Hitler—to which an estimated 300,000 residents fell victim in a period of only six weeks (1937/8) can be compared in this magnitude not only to the victims of area bombardments, but can be equated to and seen in the context of a massacre. Although it will forever be impossible to determine the exact number of victims, it is far higher than the number of people killed by the atomic bombings of Hiroshima and Nagasaki.

In a letter to Hitler, John Rabe's pleading request to intervene with the Japanese to save the residents of Nanjing not only went unanswered, but also unheard. Hitler, for many reasons, had no interest in mediation. Therefore, he is also partly to blame here.

Incidentally, five years earlier, on January 29, 1932, Shanghai was indeed the target of a Japanese area bombardment, the first against a civilian population. In 1937, not only an estimated 18,000 Chinese lost their lives, but 240,000 were made homeless [Fig.2-6]. Guernica, we recall, was not bombed extensively by the German air force until 1937, five years later.

At the end of World War II, the air warfare, which was the result of Hitler's policy of aggression, drew Dresden into its murderous vortex. Before that, it raged in countless other places, in cities outside Germany. There, it razed entire neighborhoods, sometimes almost entire cities, to the ground and cost the lives of millions of people in the process. From the abundance of air raids, we mention only a small selection here.

Fig.2-5 Chinese civilians being buried alive by Japanese invaders

Fig.2-6 Screaming young child after the bombing of Shanghai, August 28, 1937

Guernica (Spain) : During the Spanish Civil War, German fighter planes (with the participation of an Italian unit) attacked Guernica [Fig.2-7], located in the Basque Country, on April 26, 1937. The bombs, followed by a major fire, destroyed eighty percent of the buildings. Recent research suggests there were 200 to 300 casualties. Militarily relevant targets (bridges, industrial plants) were spared.

Coventry (England) : The German Luftwaffe's momentous attack on Coventry [Fig.2-8], an industrial city with a population of about 320,000 at the beginning of the war, was flown by the Luftwaffe on the evening and night of November 14, 1940. In the course of the so-called "Coventry Blitz" (with the dropping of illuminating bombs, parachute air mines, explosive and incendiary bombs with magnesium or petroleum as incendiary agents) and smaller attacks (April 8-9, 1941 and August 3, 1942), about 1,200 people had died by 1942 (568 of them in the area bombing of November 14, 1940). Terminologically, the air raid on Coventry was reflected in the word "coventrieren". This meant that a bombardment with the aim of breaking down resistance among the population and, thus, depriving the government of the consent of the population as the basis of its readiness for war.

Fig.2-7 Guernica, 1937

Fig.2-8 Coventry, 1940

London (England) : As part of the Battle of Britain and attacks on Great Britain (in English, this is referred to as "The Blitz"), the German Luftwaffe attacked London several times, particularly in the period from September 7, 1940 to May 16, 1941. The fact that an estimated 43,000 civilians died, and more than a million homes were destroyed [Fig.2-9], did nothing to bring the British government to the negotiating table, nor did it cause the government to cease its arms production. The start of the "London Blitz" on September 7, 1940, was preceded by an initial bombing of London by the German Luftwaffe on August 24, 1940, and the British Royal Air Force's response with several nighttime bombings of Berlin. The "London Blitz" was later followed by the relatively inconclusive "Baedeker Blitz" aimed at destroying culturally significant cities in England and the relatively unsuccessful "Baby Blitz" on January 21, 1944.

Fig.2-9 A London-underground-station used as the air raid shelter

Leningrad (the Soviet Union) : One of the most horrific war crimes of World War II was committed by the German Wehrmacht by systematically starving to death more than one million people in the militarily encircled Leningrad [Fig.2-10] as part of the war of extermination ordered by Hitler. The Leningrad blockade lasted from September 8, 1941, to January 27, 1944, with 16,470 civilians killed and 33,000 injured by bombs dropped (aimed at destroying mainly food warehouses and supply networks).

Warsaw (Poland): The invasion of Poland on September 1, 1939, began only a few days after the air warfare of the German Wehrmacht against Warsaw [Fig.2-11] and escalated on the so-called "bloody Sunday" (September 10, 1939) to a large-scale attack consisting of 17 individual air raids. The devastating attack in over 1,700 missions and the dropping of 560 tons of explosive and 72 incendiary bombs killed 6,000 Polish soldiers and 25,800 civilians, 16,000 soldiers and 50,000 civilians were injured, 100,000 soldiers became German prisoners of war. Poland capitulated. After the Warsaw Uprising from August 1 to October 2, 1944, German troops not only committed mass murders among the civilian population, but also destroyed 80% of the city.

Rotterdam (the Netherlands): After attacking the Hague in the morning hours of May 10, 1940, the German Luftwaffe bombed the port city of Rotterdam [Fig.2-12] in the early afternoon of May 14, 1940, with the result that the old city was completely destroyed and 814 civilians lost their lives. As a city declared a fortress city, Rotterdam could not invoke the protection of civilian installations under international law. The Dutch government capitulated. With the so-called "Rotterdam Blitz", the German Wehrmacht launches its Western campaign.

Belgrade (Serbia): If the air raid on Rotterdam marked the beginning of the Western campaign, the air raid on Belgrade (Mission Punishment) on April 6 and 7, 1941, marked the beginning of the Balkan campaign. Hitler's orders: to destroy Belgrade, the capital of Yugoslavia. Notwithstanding the declaration of the city as a so-called "Open City" (as such, it should not have been attacked or bombed, since it was not defending itself) and without a declaration of war or ultimatum, the German airborne units, together with Italian and Hungarian allies, attacked the city and destroyed it almost completely within two days [Fig.2-13]. According to official figures, over 2,000 inhabitants were killed, and 9,000 of the 20,000 houses were destroyed. As in Warsaw, the strategy was aimed at destroying the administrative and logistical center of the country. On April 16 and 17, 1944, Belgrade was also attacked for the first time by Allied bomber units.

Fig.2-10 Leningrad

Stalingrad (the Soviet Union): The siege of Stalingrad on August 23, 1942, and the offensive by German troops on September 13, 1942, marked the beginning of one of the most bitter battles of World War II. The great strategic importance of the city for the Soviet Union is no better documented than in Stalin's order "No step backwards!" at the height of the confrontation. The climax of the attack was the large-scale bombardment of Stalingrad by dive bombers combined with massive ground fighting. It was followed in the next few days by more massive air strikes with incredibly brutal close combat. By mid-October, Soviet air forces gained air superiority over Stalingrad. With the major Soviet offensive on November 19, 1942, the Battle of Stalingrad drew to a close, and on February 2, 1943, the final victory of Soviet forces ushered in the turning point in the German-Soviet War [Fig.2-14].

Fig.2-11 Warsaw

Fig.2-12 Rotterdam

Fig.2-13 Belgrad

Fig.2-14 Stalingrad city center, 1943

Counterattack—Germany in a Hail of Bombs

It is in the dynamics of dealing with a special matter that, when concentrating on the question at hand, large contexts are often faded out or temporarily put on the back burner. In the end, one will only be able to do justice to a special investigation intention if one is able to locate it in its large context and realize it from this perspective. For a look at Dresden, which was destroyed at its core through bombardment, this means: to see and understand the bombing and its terrible result in the overall context of the bombings of the anti-Hitler coalition and the effort to bring National Socialist Germany militarily to its knees in such a way that it had to stop its aggressive warlike actions. The contextualization of the study does not aim at decimating the damage by relativizing it, but at realizing its true extent. What is not required in order to adequately assess and evaluate, both in terms of its rational and ethic, the bombing of Dresden, is subjective exaggeration. Already even one casualty of war is terrible. Not a single one needs to be added, or exaggerated, in order cognitively or emotionally take position.

Informative articles on almost all air raids can now be found on the Internet, often in the formulation: "Allied air raids on (name of city)." Here we then learn more about the time of the attacks and their nature and strength, about casualty figures in detail and in comparison, of the casualty figures with the total number of inhabitants at the time of the bombing. Last but not least, we are usually informed about the degree of destruction regarding public and private buildings.

The "destruction of Dresden" is a figure of speech that is still in use today even though it is not accurate and does not describe the situation. Dresden was not destroyed completely. Dresden was destroyed in parts, especially at its core city. The newer parts of the city located on the outskirts, for example, remained almost untouched. The misleading formulation was first used in German foreign propaganda immediately after the bombing, and a short time later also in National Socialist publications and eyewitness reports. As a "common figure of speech", it was still used by journalists and nonfiction authors decades after 1945. In this context, it cannot be sufficiently pointed out that the degree of destruction in the case of Dresden was still limited compared to that of other German cities. Among many other cities, Hamburg, Pforzheim, Dortmund, Darmstadt, Krefeld, Kassel, Wurzburg, Wuppertal, Duren, Lubeck and Berlin suffered large, sometimes even major destruction. Let's take a look at the level of destruction of the following cities: Wesel 97%, Paderborn 95.6%, Bocholt 89%, Hanau 88.6%, Giessen 76.5%, Moers 75.7%, Siegen 75.3%, Emden 73.9%. Sven Felix Kellerhoff, in one of his many knowledgeable and readable contributions, not only lists these, but emphasizes that in January and February of 1944 alone, major attacks were flown on Stettin, Braunschweig, Magdeburg, Leipzig, Stuttgart, Schweinfurt, Aschaffenburg, and (six times) Berlin. The word "destruction of Dresden" (suggesting the destruction of the whole of Dresden) is irritating not only with regard to the many bombed German cities, but also and especially with regard to Coventry, London, Rotterdam, Stalingrad or Warsaw.

Besides, the fact that even Dresden could not completely rule out bombing is shown by its preventive air-raid protection measures, the establishment of services for the recovery of dead bodies, the transport of corpses and burials, and the establishment of official reporting chains, among many other things. However, it is also true that it had not prepared itself sufficiently and efficiently enough for the event of a bombing and, therefore, had to record casualties that should not have occurred at this level. The following list shows that Dresden is not an isolated case. The catastrophically widespread air raids undertaken by the Allies on German cities during World War II reflect, on the one hand, the almost desperate efforts of the anti-Hitler coalition to defeat Germany at all costs and, on the other hand, the cohesion of the population under the influence of National Socialist propaganda and the repressions of the system—notwithstanding or even as a result of the area bombings. The unbroken tenor of National Socialist war propaganda: Behold the relentless brutality of the war enemy, it does not stop at innocent children and women, nor is precious cultural property spared from it.

Let us pick out a few examples from the abundance of air raids and, in these contexts, go into the regularities of bombings (preconditions, execution, consequences). Even if most of the examples have a particularity, often a sad superlative, they describe contexts that are more or less also valid for Dresden. By taking them up in individual cases, explanations are unnecessary in connection with the description of the destructive February bombing in Dresden. The effects of area bombing and targeted destruction of militarily relevant objects (usually with not inconsiderable civilian collateral damage) are in principle comparable everywhere.

In the meantime, there are not only thorough individual studies on all air raids—all animated by the motive to record the facts and contexts as objectively as possible and supported by an increased interest of the affected cities and regions. The following examples are among those frequently mentioned. In their context, which is the guiding interest here, the aim is not to relativize the degree of destruction of Dresden, but to understand it better, i.e. against the background of the tremendous military efforts of the Allies to defeat Germany. Dresden is in every respect not a singular case, but one among a frightening number. Therefore, the bombing of Dresden, which is often highlighted among the many—as shocking as it is—does not correspond to the subjective perception with regard to its military-strategic relevance. It is especially not decisive for the war. However, it is an impressive example—representative of the many others—of the large-scale attack on a city and raises the question of how Germany was able to withstand the counterattack, which spared virtually no city, for such a long time.

What many cities have in common is that they were destroyed—as it is often emphasized—in the last two years or months, even weeks, of the war. Conversely, it can be conjectured that the end of the war can be attributed to precisely the fact of not only not abating but increasing bombardment of German cities with a massive destruction of militarily relevant infrastructure. From this point of view, the attacks on many small and large cities in the last year of the war are not regrettable superfluous counterattacks at the time of a war that was already coming to an end, but rather, according to their very intensity and scope, decisive for the war.

The Anglo-American Combined Bomber Offensive decided in the Casablanca Directive of January 21,1943, was based on the strategic war idea of increasing military pressure on Nazi Germany by combining the British Royal Air Force's (RAF) ability and willingness to carry out area bombing raids at night with the United States Army Air Force's (USAAF) ability and willingness to destroy infrastructure through systematic daylight raids on key industries, especially armaments production and fuel manufacture, transportation hubs and transport facilities. The strategy of "incendiary attacks". i.e. the specification of area-wide incendiary bombardments, had a particularly devastating effect. The British had to carry out these attacks mainly at night, since the RAF could not protect its bomber units with escort fighters as the USAAF could.

Lubeck: The air raid on Lubeck [Fig.2-15] on March 29, 1942, has gone down in the history of bombarded city centers in Germany as the first area bombing of a major German city by the British Area Bombing Directive. With the strategic decision on area bombing of February 14, 1942, the Air Force moved away from warfare focused on military objects; it had not proved particularly effective.

Cologne: Under the code name "Operation Millenium", the British Royal Air Force implemented its Trenchard Doctrine Directive for unrestricted area bombing on the night of May 30 and 31, 1942, by using more than 1,000 bombers simultaneously for the first time ("1000 bombers attack"). In this way, the RAF implemented England's painful experience with the German air forces in World War I. At that time, it had virtually nothing to oppose the Zeppelins (1915) and Gotha bombers (1917). In building a powerful air force, the RAF achieved the goal of striking at the heart of the enemy's ability and will to wage war. In Cologne, the strategy of a "bomber storm" came to full fruition for the first time through the use of bombers in large numbers, supported by a new navigation system, in conjunction with incendiary bombs. Nearly 500 people lost their lives in the process. The bombs, resulting in some 2,500 fires, caused the total or partial loss of nearly 13,000 buildings [Fig.2-16]. Between 135,000 and 150,000 of the city's then total population of 684,000 left Cologne. More often than any other city in Germany, Cologne was bombed 262 times.

Fig.2-15 Lubeck, March 29, 1942

Fig.2-16 The destroyed inner city of Cologne, 1945

Krefeld: The city center of Krefeld was reduced to ashes and rubble by more than 600 British bombers with 2,100 tons of explosive and incendiary bombs within 75 minutes during the nights of June 21 and 22, 1943 [Fig.2-17]. 1,036 people from Krefeld were killed, more than 9,000 were injured and 72,000 lost their homes. This was not the first nor the last bombardment that the city had to endure. The first bombing raid hit Krefeld in 1940, the next in 1942, and others in 1944 and 1945. The night bombing raids in particular were aimed at demoralizing the population.

Wuppertal: After the RAF dropped more than 2,000 tons of incendiary and demolition bombs over the Elberfeld district in the nights of June 24 and 25, 1943, causing firestorms, more than half of the buildings were destroyed. If one adds the air raid of May 29 and 30, 1943, a total of more than 6,500 people died and almost 40% of the city was destroyed [Fig.2-18].

Fig.2-17 Krefeld, June 21 and 22, 1943

Hamburg: The heaviest air raids in the history of air warfare up to that time cost the lives of about 34,000 people and injured an estimated 125,000 after a wave of bombings between July 24 and August 3, 1943. The so-called Operation Gomorrah (five night raids by the RAF, two day raids by the USAAF) was particularly devastating because a firestorm launched as part of it was aided by extreme weather conditions characterized by drought and heat. Air mines, demolition bombs, incendiary bombs and phosphorus bombs were used. The strategy previously tested in Lubeck of triggering large-scale fires by the combined use of different types of bombs was so successful in Hamburg from a military point of view that it was subsequently called "Hamburgization". Explosive bombs were used to destroy streets and the supply lines beneath them, and land mines were used to expose roof trusses and blow open windows and doors, so that incendiary bombs and phosphorus bombs could develop their full effect through these openings and trigger a conflagration of the greatest magnitude. Due to the unique buoyancy of the heated air masses, people and material were literally torn into the fire centers at an estimated 270 km/h.

Fig.2-18 Wuppertal, 1943

The people who fled to air-raid shelters often died—as in other cities—from toxic fire gases, especially carbon monoxide, from ruptured lungs, heat stroke, scalding and drowning, injuries caused by collapsing buildings and suffocation. Entire neighborhoods were leveled to the ground [Fig.2-19]. 277,330 homes, 580 industrial plants, 2,632 commercial enterprises, 80 military installations, 24 hospitals, 277 schools and 58 churches were destroyed. In addition, watercraft totaling 180,000 gross tons were sunk in the harbor. The name Gomorrah, borrowed from the Bible (in Genesis 19:24) to describe the military operation, captured what the "operation" intended: "Then the LORD rained down brimstone and fire from heaven on Sodom and Gomorrah." Yet it was just one hundred years ago that in May 1842 a third of Hamburg's inner city was destroyed by a firestorm that raged for days.

Kassel: Along with Hamburg, Darmstadt, Pforzheim and Dresden, Kassel [Fig.2-20] is one of the German cities that suffered the highest number of casualties in the Allied air warfare. The city was hit hardest on October 22, 1943, as part of a British Royal Air Force Bomber Command offensive.

Duren (Düren): Before Duren [Fig.2-21] was almost completely destroyed in Operation Queen on November 16, 1944, it was subjected to 51 air raids, most of them by the British Royal Air Force.

Magdeburg: After 38 air raids by a total of 5,000 bombers and the dropping of 12,500 tons of bombs between 1940 and 1945, including one of the most devastating in World War II (associated with a firestorm), on January 16, 1945, Magdeburg was one of the cities in Germany hit hardest by the Allied counterattack. 60% of Magdeburg was destroyed, the city center almost completely in ruins [Fig.2-22]. Between 5,000 and 6,000 people were killed (others estimate 2,500 dead, not 16,000 as claimed) by the SED (Socialist Unity Party of Germany, also known as the East German Communist

Fig.2-19 Hamburg

Fig.2-20 Kassel, Octorber 22, 1943

Fig.2-21 Market Square in Duren, 1944

Fig.2-22 Magdeburg

Party) during the GDR, the number of missing and wounded was in the thousands, and well over 200,000 people were left homeless. At the same time, there were strong air-raid-preparedness services, numerous air-raid shelters with corresponding seats and berths, an elaborate underground network of connections and escape routes, 6,000 breaches of firewalls alone, a fire department reinforced by even volunteer women, a belt of anti-aircraft positions to protect military installations, armaments factories, and traffic routes, as well as fighter planes stationed close to the city for air defense. If any city had to face attacks, it was Madgeburg, with numerous new barracks, a strong industry (including armaments industry, aircraft and engine plants, a power station), and significant transport networks (not least a large port).

Berlin: In addition to RAF and USAAF, the Soviet, as well as the French, took part in the 310 attacks on Berlin, some of which included 40 heavy air raids and 29 large-scale attacks. The attacks took place in the period from June 7, 1940 to March 18, 1945, with the three largest being flown on February 3 and 26 and March 18, 1945. In all, more than 45,000 tons of bombs were dropped over the city [Fig.2-23], more in total than on any other German city. An estimated 50,000 people, most of them civilians, lost their lives. Many died even in air raid shelters under falling building sections, suffocated, burned or drowned in firefighting water. Unlike the soldiers, the civilians could not surrender and in this way at least save their lives.

Fig.2-23 Berlin, French Street (Französische Straße)

Pforzheim: Measured against its population of about 80,000 (1939), Pforzheim suffered the highest number of air war casualties in the then German Reich, with nearly 18,000 victims of a mere 22-minute raid by 379 British Royal Air Force bombers on February 23, 1945. In a few minutes, a third of the population died. The British Royal Air Force's moral bombing, which destroyed 98% of the city, had a particularly catastrophic effect on Pforzheim because the city, with its narrow, winding streets, consisted of numerous easily half-timbered houses [Fig.2-24].

Dortmund: At the height of the air war, the British Royal Air Force's air raid on Dortmund on March 12, 1945, with more than 1,000 bombers, set the sad record for the heaviest air raid carried out in Europe. Dortmund's city center had already been completely destroyed by a major raid from October 6 to 7, 1944, more than 4,800 tons of explosive and mine bombs finished the city off [Fig.2-25]. This bombardment was also aimed at breaking the war morale of the population. In concrete terms, however, it was also and especially directed at the Ruhr region as the "arms factory" of the National Socialist Reich. The armaments factories concentrated in the Ruhr region and the corresponding transport routes were to be destroyed, thus making it impossible for the German military to obtain supplies. To this day, the Ruhr region is still suffering from the destruction caused by the war and so-called contaminated sites.

Wurzbrug (Würzburg): Wurzbrug, like many other large cities, was bombed shortly before the end of World War II. After a bombing raid by the British Bomber Command on March 16, 1945, which lasted no longer than 20 minutes, not only was 90% of the historic old town destroyed [Fig.2-26], but above all up to 5,000 people had lost their lives in it. What the people of Wurzburg have in common with Dresden is that until March 1945 they were still under the illusion that they had been spared a major attack. In fact, Wurzbrug was still on the list of cities to be bombed when the Allies threatened to run out of targets. It was also possible that an entry by Winston Churchill in the city's *Golden Book* (1909) saved it from an earlier bombardment. The inhabitants felt safe mainly because Wurzburg was home to hospitals instead of a significant armaments industry.

Fig.2-24 Pforzheim, February 23, 1945

Fig.2-25 Dortmund central train station in October 1944 after a bombing raid and the victims of the same lined up on the street.

Fig.2-26 Wurzburg, 1945

The fact that the devastating February bombing of Dresden has focused attention on air raids should not obscure the reality that the war was not fought solely and not decisively in the air, but also and especially on the ground, by and large through concerted actions by the Army, Air Force and Navy. The major offensive of the Western Allies carried out in 1944 as part of Operation Overlord (with its history-making D-Day) ultimately cost the lives of well over 100,000 soldiers (not counting the missing), 65,000 on the side of the anti-Hitler coalition, 50,000 on the side of Hitler's forces. On the Allied side alone, 155,000 were wounded, and meanwhile 200,000 German soldiers were taken prisoner of war. The Allied troops with about 1,530,000 soldiers were opposed by the German army with about 350,000 soldiers.

Everyday War Life

Since the Nazi regime endeavored from the beginning of the war to demand as few sacrifices as possible from the population—in the interest of a positive war morale—and to make possible as far-reaching a normality of everyday life as possible, there were no stunning changes in the lives of the population, even if one might have feared otherwise against the background of the relatively fresh memories of World War I and the deprivations that accompanied it (the following remarks are mainly based on an article by A. Scriba, which summarizes everyday life in World War II in a formative way). Nevertheless, with the increasing number of air raids, concern for one's own life joined the concern for one's relatives at the front. The propagandistic emphasis on the so-called home front and the appeal to the solidarity of the (especially female) population with the soldiers on the war front did nothing to change this.

However, the wounds inflicted by World War I were still too fresh for the entry into the war to be met with enthusiasm among the population. Since the hunger years of 1916 to 1919, which were due to a miserable shortage of food supply, were still fresh in the minds of the urban population in particular, and the rural population was still aware of the withdrawal of manpower and the requisitioning of horses for the war, the Reich Defense Council had already regulated the rationing of various supplies (including food, fuel and coal) in detail in 1937—so as not to give any unnecessary cause for demoralization in the future. The fact that there was no shortage of grain and potatoes, sugar and meat at the beginning of the war was due to abundant harvests in the two previous years. The compulsory rationing introduced successively at the start of the war initially affected lard, meat, butter, milk, cheese, sugar and jam. These were available from September 1, 1939, and bread and eggs from September 25, 1939, only against ration cards. To purchase rationed textiles, civilians needed a ration card (Reichskleiderkarte) valid for one year from mid-October 1939, with a total of 100 points: 4 points, for example, for a pair of stockings; 25 for a sweater; or 45 for a woman's blouse. Increasingly, the diet was based primarily on potatoes, legumes, flour and sugar; coffee was replaced by a coffee substitute made from barley or acorns; cakes were baked from carrots and potatoes, and jam was made from turnips. Even though the quality of bread declined, it was rationed to 2,250 grams per week during the first two years of the war, meat to 500 grams and fat to 270 grams, and only heavy workers, expectant mothers or children could receive whole milk (while others had to make do with skim milk). Thanks to special allowances, there were "no serious nutritional problems" primarily because the occupied territories were "ruthlessly exploited" and a supply strategy was pursued that included "death by starvation" in Eastern Europe.

> *Jews, on the other hand, also experienced severe discrimination and public humiliation in the system used to acquire food and textiles. Compared to the non-Jewish population, Jews were allotted significantly fewer calories for their ration cards in the stores intended for them. Persecution and disenfranchisement of Jews had increased markedly in severity with the onset of the war in Germany. Medical care for Jews existed only in rudimentary form. Gradually, they were banned from owning radios, telephones, motor vehicles and pets. In order to be publicly identified as a Jewish "enemy of the Reich", every Jew over the age of six, beginning on September 19, 1941, had to wear a yellow star [Fig.2-27] clearly visible on his or her clothing [Fig.2-28].*

Fig.2-27 Yellow badge / Jewish badge

Fig.2-28 Man with Jewish badge

In order to keep wartime morale stable among the population, consumer goods were produced and provided at prewar levels. To prevent anti-war sentiment from arising, women were initially not conscripted into service and the utilization of their labor potential was comparatively minimal (different from Great Britain and the America). This restraint was compensated for by the work of forced laborers and prisoners of war, as well as by the transfer of women from disused factories and fields of work that had little significance for the war to systemically relevant ones, i.e. those affecting agriculture, the war economy, and the administrative sector. Beginning in 1939, female youths were required to perform six months of Reich labor service, which was extended by another six months beginning in 1941 as "war relief service" in air-raid protection, social institutions, families with many children, or transportation companies (for example, streetcars). Equal pay for women and men in armaments factories, improvements in worker and maternity protection, and state welfare benefits served to compensate for deteriorating working conditions and longer working hours of up to 50 hours per week.

Instead of attending school, children and young people—organized by the schools or the Hitler Youth—were assigned to harvesting missions in the countryside. They were used, among other, to pick up potato beetles or to perform distributive tasks, as well as to collect leaflets and incendiary plaques dropped from planes of the Allied troops. The incendiary flakes, which contained moistened phosphorus and ignited after drying out, were intended to set grain crops ablaze and destroy them. Within the framework of the "War Winter Relief" (Kriegswinterhilfswerk) and of collections of old school materials, the pupils were assigned to collect old paper, cloth or metals as a contribution to the "people's community" (Volksgemeinschaft). Since the pupils missed a lot of school during this time, they received the so-called "emergency Abitur" instead of the Abitur.

For the armaments factories, an appeal was made from April 1940 for "metal donations" and, in view of the frostbite suffered by Wehrmacht soldiers on the Eastern Front, beginning with the winter of 1941, winter clothing (mainly coats and furs, but also overshoes, socks, sweaters, undervests, body bandages, head and ear protectors, leather and knitted gloves, scarves, shoe inserts, etc.) as well as blankets and "generally everything that serves to fight the winter cold which set in so early this year" were collected. The whole thing was declared as "Christmas gift from the homeland for our soldiers" and the individual donations were receipted and certified with a certificate [Fig.2-29].

> Certificate
>
> In the name of the Fuehrer, I thank Mr. Peter Ring for the donation towards the collection of wool, fur and winter clothing for the battle front.
>
> Dr. Goebbels,
> Reich Propaganda Leader and Reich Minister for Public Enlightenment and Propaganda, Christmas, 1941

Fig.2-29 Certification of donation with respect to the 1941 winter collection of goods

Regardless of the turmoil of war, or even because of it, people sought diversion and distraction. They listened to the radio or read. They consumed war-glorifying literature, listened to the war reports, pop songs and, above all, the greeting broadcast regularly followed by half of the population at a time in the interest of linking the war front and the home front (Wunschkonzert für die Wehrmacht) that was broadcast every Sunday. The song "Lili Marleen", first performed by Lale Andersen in Norbert Schultze's version in 1941, sparked emotions like no other songs. As a soldier's anthem, it quickly became an international classic. Regardless of the danger of becoming a target of air raids, the masses flocked to stadiums to attend soccer matches. Cinema played a major role. Through the radio broadcast "The German Weekly Review" (Wochenschau), war successes were regularly reported. To this day, however, the actors who were popular during the Third Reich (among them, for example, Heinz Rühmann, Hans Moser or Marika Rökk, Zarah Leander and Ilse Werner) are still the subject of critical discussion with regard to their participation in maintaining wartime morale through corresponding film offers and their role model function (one of the best-known influencers for the ladies of the time was Ilse Werner). They played roles in deliberately apolitical entertainment films serving mere diversion, for example *The Punch Bowl* (*Die Feuerzangenbowle*) in 1944. In the first year of the war alone, the film industry counted over one billion moviegoers.

From 1942 onward, people in the cities increasingly had to seek out air-raid shelters after an air-raid alarm and protect themselves against smoke by means of "people's gas masks". Evacuations became more frequent, sometimes on a large scale. Children were sent to the countryside for their safety and also for recreation, known in German as "Kinderlandverschickung". In 1943 alone, over 700,000 people left Berlin and sought shelter in the countryside. Bombed out, many had to rely on emergency quarters. Because paper became scarce, print media often appeared only as special editions. Many goods could only be obtained on the black market, which was actually forbidden but nevertheless flourished. Although this did not lead to widespread rebellion, the fact that the party bigwigs (including Hitler) enjoyed privileges was by no means overlooked by the population. While in the summer of 1940 the victory over the "archenemy" France was still celebrated, in the course of the occupation the soldiers were also strongly persuaded by the French way of life and so adopted it (B. Wegner). The sympathy for the country and its people was later to form a not insignificant basis for the friendship that developed between France and Germany.

With the surrender of Hitler's army at Stalingrad and the defeat of the Germans in the German-Italian African campaign, a war weariness gradually developed, but expressing it was severely punished. After the defeat in Stalingrad, panic seized the Nazi regime, Goebbels proclaimed the "total war" with the consequence that now all available materials and human resources were mobilized, all enterprises and businesses that were not relevant to the war were closed, large parts of the population were obliged to work in armament fields, and all men fit for military service were deployed as soldiers, members of the Waffen-SS, or as policemen.

Now even 14-to-18-year-old Hitler Youth boys were trained in military training camps and drafted as soldiers. From 1943, 15-year-olds had to replace anti-aircraft soldiers as "air force helpers" (Luftwaffenhelfer) and from the fall of 1944, in the context of the proclamation of the "Volkssturm" (national militia established by the Nazi Party), even had to engage in trench warfare. For the youths, this often ended fatally. The advance of the Red Army was preceded by a flight of people from East Prussia and Saxony to the West. "In the west of the Reich, on the other hand, the British and Americans were mostly greeted warmly, not so much as 'liberators' from the Nazi regime, but out of relief that they were moving in ahead of the Red Army as occupiers and that the war, which had been full of losses and had brought death to some 3.8 to 4 million German soldiers and 1.65 million civilians, would now soon come to an end." (B. Wegner). This does not mean that there was no fear in the West regarding the end of the war and its consequences for the German people. "Not infrequently, in the spring of 1945, a strangely bizarre doomsday mood prevailed, and those who until then had also been materially privileged, such as functionaries or officers, celebrated it with alcohol orgies, while a large part of the population, especially in the cities and refugees, had trouble getting enough to eat or finding a roof over their heads." Of course, even after the end of the war, people in some cases continued to suffer from the accompanying circumstances and consequences of the war for years. In every respect, the population of Dresden and its Saxon surroundings did not fare any differently here than anyone else in the Third Reich.

The February Bombing

At the time of the bombing of Dresden, the air raids had long since been directed not only at military objects and the armaments industry in particular and, beyond that, at industrial plants in general and the entire infrastructure, especially traffic, but also—specifically—at the population. Civilian casualties among the population were not regarded as regrettable collateral damage and accepted as such, but were instead strategically included as a declared target of bombing, especially by the British Royal Air Force. Indeed, there is no other way to put it: this was done deliberately. Corresponding guidelines can be found in the "Area Bombing Directive" issued on February 14, 1942. The ethical side of a war strategy that was not only demanded and formulated in this way, but also practiced across the board, will be discussed below.

When speaking about the bombing of Dresden, what is usually being referred to is the bombing in February 1945, just before the end of the war. It is certainly a special and particularly memorable one for various reasons. But it is not the only one that hit Dresden. The fact that Dresden had already been bombed on August 24, 1944 (here, mainly industrial facilities were hit and a total of 241 people were killed), as well as on October 7, 1944 (in this attack, among others on a defense company and a railroad station, 270 people died) and January 16, 1945 (in the process, 334 people lost their lives, and again, the target was a train station), shows that Dresden was definitely and fundamentally "worth bombing" in terms of military strategy. After all, Dresden was, not only towards the end of the war, in addition to its armaments industry and militarily relevant facilities and installations, an important transportation juncture and thus also a military transshipment point in the southeast of the German Reich (with excellent train connections to Berlin, Leipzig, Nuremberg, Prague and Warsaw). Another significant fact with regard to Dresden's military strategic importance: Dresden was bombed even after the destructive effects of the February bombing, both on March 2 and April 17—primarily with the aim of destroying railroad facilities. In almost all cases, explosive and incendiary bombs were used. Here is an overview of the quantity:

Table 2-1 Type and Quantity of Bombs used by the Allies in the Dresden bombing

Time	Type and Quantity of Bombs
Oct. 7, 1944 (12:34-12:36)	70 tons of explosive bombs
Jan. 16, 1945 (12:12-12:17)	264 tons of explosive bombs, 41 tons of incendiary bombs
Feb. 13/14, 1945 (22:03-22:28)	1,447 tons of blockbuster bombs and explosive bombs, 1,181 tons of incendiary bombs
Feb. 14, 1945 (12:17-12:38)	474 tons of blockbuster bombs and explosive bombs
Feb. 15, 1945 (11:51-12:01)	463 tons of explosive bombs
Mar. 2, 1945 (10:27-11:03)	940 tons of explosive bombs
Apr. 17, 1945 (13:48-15:12)	1,554 tons of explosive bombs, 164 tons of incendiary bombs

In order to be able to correctly classify the bombardment carried out in February from a purely strategic military point of view, this bombardment and the one carried out before and after February 13, 14 and 15 must be included. Only the whole ensemble of bombardments underlines the military relevance of "Florence on the Elbe". They hit everything else but the "innocent", which, if emphasized here, should not excuse them, and which were specifically directed against the civilian population, but, following a military-strategic immanent logic, should make the bombardments at least comprehensible. From the point of view of military strategy alone, Dresden deserved to be bombed no less than the other cities of belligerent Germany. Here, however, it should also be noted that experts do not agree on whether area bombing in general and the area bombing of Dresden, not least at its late date, can be regarded as meaningful solely from the point of view of military strategy. In any case, the wave of attacks by USAAF integrated into the February bombardment, which followed the first wave of attacks by RAF that triggered the firestorm, is generally regarded as completely superfluous from a military point of view. Therefore, there are not only ethical concerns.

Circumstances

Since the side that has the greatest chance of winning the war is the one that knows how to maintain the social infrastructure over the longest period of time, military and civil defense (warfare) are two sides of one and the same coin. Among the numerous measures of civil defense, bunker construction, i.e. protection of the population mainly from bombardment, is a central one. Accordingly, Hitler's war strategy included the construction of air raid shelters and corresponding decrees. However efficient the bunkers were, both in individual cases and in terms of war strategy in general, they were also essentially aimed at the war morale of the population. The bunkers promise and actually suggest protection and above all, that those politically responsible will take care of the population even in hard times. The same applies to the military and civilian medical system, alongside the motive of sincere compassion and corresponding precautions. By being prepared to take appropriate rescue measures in an emergency and having facilities (clinics) where those affected can be treated, wartime policy gives citizens, and not least its soldiers, the reassuring feeling that they will not be left alone in personally difficult times. To a limited extent, the facilities actually benefit those affected, since people can survive a bombardment by escaping into air raid shelters, and soldiers can receive sanitary or clinical care.

Against the background of these contexts, it must now be stated, with a particular view to the nationwide air raid protection specifications, that those responsible in Dresden—Dresden had a population of around 630,000 at the beginning of World War II—had done little to protect the city against the effects of a bombing. An exception to this was the head district administrator ("Gauleiter"), who even had an air raid shelter built for himself and a few privileged people from the party and administration in his private garden. Although an air raid had to be expected, the head district administrator and others "hoped"—against all reasons—that it would not happen. They buried their heads in the sand at the expense of the populace and left them largely unprotected against later attacks. Worse even, they talked down the danger, were deceptive about it and reassured the populace with false facts, even then when Leipzig, a major city in Saxony, was left in a devastated state after being bombed for the first time in December 1943. Until the first devastating wave of attacks, the populace itself, by and large, gave in to the self-deception that Dresden had a kind of special role in the war and was somehow an exception. It can, therefore, rightly be said that had appropriate air protection measures been put into place, the number of casualties caused by the bombings that followed could probably have been reduced.

Conversely, air raid shelters of all kinds, whether bunkers, designated air raid shelters or cellars suitable for air raid protection, can become traps for those seeking shelter in them.

Exits, cellar stairs, windows and air shafts can be buried or blocked after being hit by a bomb, with the result that those trapped there die an agonizing death by suffocation, burning, scalding (extinguishing water) or starvation. In most cases, the tragedy already begins in the course of searching for and occupying shelters, when in the hectic rush and due to lack of space, due to frailty, the strong prevail over the weak and solidary action succumbs to selfish action.

Sequence of Events

When World War II—as we know today, but could not say with absolute certainty at that time—was coming to an end, about eleven weeks earlier, Dresden met the fate that had struck numerous cities in Germany before—often far more massively: Dresden became the target of an extensive and intensive bombardment, in this case by a military task force of RAF with 759 bombers on the one side and USAAF with about 500 bombers on the other. From the evening of February 13 to noon on February 15, 1945, and within a long 37 hours and in the course of four waves of attacks, the British-American units dropped an estimated 2,400 tons of high explosive bombs and 1,500 incendiary bombs on the core of the historic old city, as well as on military and industrial installations scattered in various parts of the city.

To be noted is that February 14 marks a special anniversary: on this exact day three years earlier—February 14, 1942—the British Air Ministry issued the Area Bombing Directive. As commander of the British Royal Air Force Bomber Command appointed at the same time, Arthur Harris resolutely implemented the directive. The military strategy directive primarily involved the bombing of areas, i.e. cities, in particular inner cities and residential areas, and thus explicitly civilian targets, or more precisely, the population. In this way, it implemented the intention—still questionable today from the point of view of both military efficiency and ethical responsibility—of shaking the morale of the population in such a way that it would urge its government to abandon its wartime actions. Specifically, one consideration involved the idea of bombing the residential quarters of industrial workers instead of individual armaments factories and war-relevant enterprises in order to keep them from their work activities and to impair or make the production of war goods along the way impossible. The same applied to infrastructure.

In terms of military strategy, Dresden was interesting not only as an important transportation hub for rail connections to Berlin, Leipzig, Nuremberg, Warsaw and Prague, and thus specifically for troop transfers to the Eastern Front, but also because of its armament factories scattered throughout the city, not least its aircraft facilities. Dresden was therefore by no means what many thought of it then and how some still think of it today—an "innocent cultural beauty".

When the air raid alarm sounded in Dresden for the 175th time at 21:45 on February 13, 1945 (Shrove Tuesday), the people—in the absence of air raid shelters—sought protection against an air raid primarily in cellars of their homes, without suspecting, let alone knowing, that their city was about to be subjected to a historic attack.

15 minutes later, at 22:03 a British Royal Air Force "Pathfinder" unit using Lancaster bombers [Fig.2-30] dropped so-called "Christmas trees" (magnesium light cascades) to illuminate the city center. Two minutes later, nine RAF De Havilland Mosquitos [Fig.2-31] dropped red target markers. They served to guide the 244 Lancaster bombers that followed with a view to dropping an initial 529 blockbuster bombs and 1,800 explosive and incendiary bombs weighing a total of 900 tons. The bombing lasted from 22:13 to 22:28. These 15 minutes were enough to set three quarters of the old city ablaze. Pinpoint bombing was not intended.

This was not enough. Oriented toward the source of the fire, another 529 Lancaster bombers of the British and Canadian air forces dropped 650,000 incendiary bombs (exactly 648,586 thermite incendiaries) weighing a total of 1,500 tons between 01:23 and 01:54 as part of a second wave of attacks. These also hit those who had sought shelter outdoors, on the Elbe meadows or in the Grand Garden. The bomb craters and the large fire, which consisted of many individual fires, made firefighting almost impossible.

Over the nightly work of destruction carried out by RAF on the night of February 13 to 14, the involvement of USAAF is often overlooked. It flew a daytime attack under cloudy skies on February 14, exactly from 12:17 to 12:31, with more than 300 B-17 Bombers [Fig.2-32] flanked by 100 to 200 escort fighters, on a target radar basis, unloading 1,800 high explosive bombs (with a total weight of 474 tons) and 136,800 incendiary bombs with a total weight of 296 tons over individual armament factories, the Friedrich City railroad station and the Dresden Reichsbahn repair plant. The fact that a hospital and parts of the city were hit in the process was probably understood more as collateral damage from the American point of view at the time—and also because one of their bomber units confused Prague with Dresden.

Another daytime raid was flown by the American Air Force, this time with 211 B-17 Bombers on the following day, February 15, 1945, again at noon, between 11:51 to 12:01. Due to poor visibility, the pilots dropped 460 tons of bombs over the neighboring areas of Dresden, the area between Meissen and Pirna.

In order to understand the degree and extent of destruction, knowledge of explosive and incendiary bombs, their usage, especially their sequence of usage and their specific effects is essential.

The aim of incendiary bombs (often weighing no more than 2 kg, but sometimes several hundred kilograms) is to set fire to buildings and the like as precisely as possible, but also over a wide area, by bursting on the ground and releasing incendiary agents that are difficult to extinguish. If the intensity or extent of their use is high, they can, for example in Hamburg, cause firestorms and as a result, due to the high temperatures, in addition to the fires they start, lead to death by drawing air and thus oxygen from the side streets of a fire center and the buildings located there through a hurricane-like, thermal suction effect with such force that people die through suffocation or dehydration.

Fig.2-30 Lancester

Fig.2-31 De Havilland Mosquito

Fig.2-32 B-17 Bomber

The firestorm as a war technique developed by the German Air Force was used for the first time in the air raid "Operation Moonlight Sonata" on Coventry on Nov 14 and 15, 1940, then among other things in the attack on Manchester on Christmas 1940. 500 bombers dropped about 1,500 tons of bombs on Coventry. After the British Royal Air Force had adopted the technique, it was first used in the attack on Lubeck on March 28 and 29, 1942, and finally also in its air raid on Hamburg as part of its "Operation Gomorrha" from July 24 to August 3, 1943, with over 30,000 casualties. In addition to the devastating effects of the RAF's strategy of large-scale bombing with incendiary bombs, usually carried out in several waves in quick succession, the devastating use of incendiary bombs in the bombing of Tokyo by USAAF on August 3, 1945, with more than 80,000 fatalities, is likely to be among the most consequential. If phosphorus canisters are used as accelerants in incendiary bombing raids, the effects are particularly devastating.

In particular, the relatively small incendiary bombs, of which the British Royal Air Force used more than 80 million in its bombardments against Germany, would not be effective if they were not preceded by the dropping of explosive bombs or blockbuster bombs. Their effect was essentially to generate an enormous blast wave with their detonation, causing widespread devastation—hence the name "(apartment) blockbuster". People who were in the vicinity of the explosion hearth died instantly from the pressure exerted on their lungs.

Blockbusters, such as the HC Blockbuster [Fig.2-33] used in World War II, which looks similar to a water tank and weighs two tons with its 1,400 kilograms of explosives, had to, as part of a first wave of attacks, blow up parts of buildings, especially roof trusses, so that incendiary bombs could enter into them and set them on fire in a subsequent wave of attacks. To ensure that the incendiary bombs explode on the surface and rather than fizzle out below it, they were often equipped with a nose-rod of about 100 cm length, which made contact with the target, triggering the explosion already before actual impact. Blockbusters also had the use of rendering roads and locations inaccessible to relief transports. Incendiary bombs cannot be rendered harmless and fires cannot be extinguished; the injured cannot be rescued and the dead cannot be recovered.

Fig.2-33 HC-4000 unexploded ordnance (1,790 kg)

The Aftermath

The aftermath of the incendiary bombs was devastating. The core of Dresden's "Old Town" was completely destroyed over an area of 15 square kilometers, except for a few badly damaged buildings. Individual parts of the city were also badly hit, largely burned down and destroyed. 80,000 of 220,000 homes fell victim to the bombing. Overnight, the "cultural beauty", the "Florence on the Elbe" had become a field of ruins and rubble. Through wall breakthroughs in houses hit by bombs, some of the survivors were able to escape into other houses, or managed to get out into the open and to flee into other parts of the city which were less or not at all affected by the bombing, as well as into the areas surrounding Dresden. 1,000 people found shelter in a church. Many burned to death; many succumbed to heat shock, the high air pressure, or suffocated from fumes due to lack of ventilation in the makeshift shelters. Many of those who fled into the open were victims of the firestorm or bomb blasts. Families were torn apart by the bombing chaos. Many survived the bomb terrors deeply traumatized. About 70 Jews, however, were saved by the bombing and the chaos that accompanied it. They were able to flee Dresden without being pursued by the Gestapo, whose central building had been destroyed. Others who had taken shelter later fled the city. Forty other Jews, nonetheless, died as a result of bombs hitting the "ghetto house" (Judenhaus).

In his report to the government in Berlin of March 15, 1945—that is, four weeks after the bombing—the Dresden police chief reported the number of 18,375 killed as of March 10, 1945, but did not rule out, based on experience in connection with the recovery of the dead, that in the end about 25,000 were to be expected. On March 31, 1945, the number of deaths was corrected to 22,096.

Immediately after the waves of attacks, reception centers were set up for 16,000 refugees, food supplies for the survivors were organized, dead bodies were recovered, and due to fear of an epidemic outbreak, corpses were collected and burned in public squares, among them 6,865 in the Old Market, and in a crematorium. All in all, 10,430 dead bodies and the ashes from the cremations were buried. Those who could not be accommodated in the provisional emergency camps for the homeless were taken to the surrounding countryside. Soon the food supply collapsed, and the population was left to fend for itself. The Nazi Party was unable to work, numerous civil servants had perished or fled, and day-to-day administrative tasks could no longer be performed. Seventy-five percent of the streetcar overhead lines had been destroyed, and the streets were largely impassable due to 1,100 bomb craters. In order to reach their workplaces or town council offices, citizens mostly had to move through deserts of rubble. While the long-distance routes through Dresden, which were highly relevant militarily for the transport of troops to the East, had remained largely intact until the next bombing on March 2, 1945, it took two weeks to repair regional rail traffic. Most businesses had to shut down.

The following compilation of photos conveys—purely visually and related to buildings—an impression of the work of destruction. The suffering associated with the destruction, however, can only be approximated by us outsiders. No imagination, however vivid, can rationally or emotionally grasp the reality of a bombardment and its physical and psychological damage. Only the dead and those directly involved in the bombing could do so. It might, nonetheless, still be difficult for them to put the whole thing into words in such a way that the listener would be able to adequately comprehend the content of the narration and to get an idea of what had happened.

In addition to Church of Our Lady, which was destroyed down to its foundation walls during the war (it collapsed, delayed by a few hours, at 10:15 on February 15, 1945, as a result of the bombing), other well-known major objects of destruction include the Semper Opera House, the Royal Palace and Zwinger. [Fig.2-34 to Fig.2-49]

Fig.2-34 Dresden. View from the Town Hall Tower to the south with the Allegory of Kindness (also: Bonitas Sculpture by August Schreitmüller, created 1908-1910), photographed 1945

Fig.2-35 View from the tower of the Cross Church onto the city center of Dresden destroyed by the air raids, 1945

Fig.2-37 View from the Tower of the New Town Hall

Fig.2-36 View from the Town Hall Tower to the northwest

Fig.2-39 Destroyed city center of Dresden

Fig.2-38 View from the Town Hall Tower over the destroyed city center onto the towers of the St. Johns Church (Johanneskirche) and the Trinity Church (Trinitatiskirche)

Fig.2-40 View onto the destroyed city sections Johannstadt and Pirnaische Vorstand: the middle depicts the ruins of the Gewandhaus; bottom right the roofs of the Town Hall; middle of left side is the Old Country House, photo taken ca. 1950

Fig.2-41 Emperor Palace (Pirnaischer Platz with Kaiserpalast) in ruins

Fig.2-42 Church of Our Lady, 1965

Fig.2-43 Catholic Dresden Cathedral with destroyed vault and roof

Fig.2-44 Dresden Old Town, New Market in ruins

Fig.2-45 Destroyed Chimes Pavillion in Zwinger, view onto Hausmannsturm

Fig.2-46 Wallpavillion in Zwinger, September 1945

Fig.2-47 Outer view of Semper Opera House, directly after World War II

Fig.2-48 Inner view of Semper Opera House, directly after World War II

Fig.2-49 Outer view of Taschenberg Palace, after World War II

The panorama of ruins makes it clear: not just one house was hit by an aerial bomb, but an entire area was bombed to rubble. That's the way modern war is, everywhere. That's how it is on the other side, on the side of the "enemy". And so it is in Aleppo. The images are interchangeable. People who have not lost their lives and have even been spared from wounds, but who had lost their belongings, the roof over their heads, their hard-earned possessions. How much will and strength, how much psychological and physical strength are required to rise again from misery and overcome it? If we want to know what the word "hullabaloo" means, we have to look at the fields of ruins of World War II.

Even if a large part of the movable cultural assets could be moved out of storage in time and thus escaped the destruction of the war, the bloodletting of art in Dresden was immense. The extent of the destruction of architectural monuments is obvious and does not require a closer look. And yet, what is this in comparison with the people who lost their lives in the area bombing, indeed, with even a single person among the many? What does the loss of unique historical buildings and paintings mean compared to that of human lives? Since the meticulous investigations of a commission of historians appointed by the city of Dresden, there is no longer any reasonable doubt that the number of deaths related to the bombing ranges between approximately 22,000 and 25,000.

Because not least and especially the dead in the mass reflect the reality of the bombardment, they are to be recalled and appreciated here—obeying the pure pragmatism of hygiene and therefore indiscriminately piled up into a heap of lifeless beings for burning—by appropriate visual material [Fig.2-50]. Obviously, wars always have the same face: piles of corpses like the one in Dresden characterize most war theater, the focal point being the contempt for humanity typical of war.

Fig.2-50 The burning of corpses

And where are those who were able to escape death and survived the attack [Fig.2-51], but hundreds of thousands of whom have to fight a battle for life as war-disabled people with the most severe injuries to body and soul—often left to their own devices, a burden for their relatives and society, survivors, but losers nonetheless? Even if the term did not exist at that time, the clinical pictures already did: that of the traumatized soldier and that of the traumatized civilian. Many coped through self-medicating with alcohol. What else could they do? And the physically disabled helped themselves with prostheses and walking aids and arranged themselves in such a way so as to manage as best they could without one or the other of their limbs.

Fig.2-51 War-disabled people with amputated legs from World War II

Military medical developments also made it possible to save soldiers, some of whom were seriously wounded. Gunshot and stab wounds could be increasingly better treated, many a soldier owed his survival to antiseptic wound care in field hospitals and clinics, and the introduction of steel helmets to protect against head injuries (in the German Wehrmacht from 1916) reduced the fatal consequences of gunshots to the head. However, these and other developments also led to a correspondingly large number of war-disabled soldiers (half a million in Germany after World War I, one and a half million after World War II): People with amputated limbs, with disfigured faces, with brain injuries, with hearing and visual impairments, and not least with psychological wounds and challenges.

A special feature of total war is its consequences for civilians: they are increasingly involved in the fighting and are therefore also its victims, and comparatively more so than the soldiers themselves. For this reason, civilians, not least children, are among the state-recognized war-disabled. In 2000, 372,069 war-disabled people in Germany were still entitled to state benefits. Added to this today are those military servicemen who became disabled as a result of military missions abroad (e.g., Afghanistan).

Even though the farmer had already thoroughly harvested his field and was certainly sure not to miss any potato, an army of mostly women stormed the same field in the hopes of finding potatoes that had been missed—a nearly hopeless endeavor [Fig.2-52]. How great must the hunger and despair be of people who struggle for their survival in this way? The degradation of humans—as the accompanying photo impressively shows—does not end with the end of war, it extends far beyond.

Fig.2-52 Searching for potatoes after harvesting on the outskirts of Dresden, ca. 1946

Symbolization

The fact that the bombing of Dresden, of all places, could become the epitome of the inferno of a war is reflected not only by authors who deal with the bombing in a particularly intensive way. Whoever studies the effects of World War II in its extensiveness and intensity either stumbles over the much-used phrase "like Dresden" as, upon closer examination, an inappropriate attribution or just uncritically accepts it as such. In fact, other cities in Germany, but first and foremost in the attacked foreign countries, suffered from the consequences of an air raid much more than Dresden had. Nevertheless, Dresden is generally considered to be the city that was particularly affected by the war. The search for an answer to the question of how Dresden came to have its "image" is a broad one.

Dresden should foremost be seen as a historically significant city of culture, located in the idyllic Elbe River landscape. Dresden's considerable historical significance is underscored by the fact that this city, in conjunction with the unique Elbe valley and its buildings classified as historical landmarks, was once recognized as a UNESCO World Cultural Heritage Site (however, it was only because of an unfortunate construction measure that the city was stripped of its title after only a few years). Dresden and culture were synonymous before the military destruction of its core. But it was not only within Germany that Dresden was considered a haven for the cultivation of culture. Dresden had set cultural standards over the centuries, so much so that it was regarded worldwide as the city of fine arts and Baroque architecture, and with a widespread view of it as the occidental capital of culture. That now—following the destruction of numerous other German cities—this culturally so highly valued Dresden should also be attacked, and that, out of all things, the unique historical city center should be targeted and completely destroyed was more than not only Dresden's unsuspecting and unprepared population could fathom or process. The enormity of this tragedy and loss can only be measured and understood in relation to the immeasurable cultural value of what has been destroyed. The destruction of Dresden's cultural core was perceived and described as so incomparably massive that it became the benchmark for the destruction of other cities. Last but not least, since Dresden had, as an impressive cultural capital, always been more in the focus of general attention, its destruction generated more public and global attention than that of other cities had.

Actually, the attack, which is always to be understood as a counterattack of the British-American bomber group, should not have caught the population of Dresden unprepared. While the Gauleiter of the city (head district administrator) had himself built a bunker under his private house, the population had to face the attack without comparable protection. Against the requirement to take air protection measures, the Gauleiter had relied on nonsensical military defense measures. Given this fact, indications that (considerably) fewer people would have had to give up their lives if appropriate air raid protection measures had been taken are certainly not unfounded.

Dresden was also simply shocked by the attack. Although it had already been attacked militarily before, it had been all too aware of the time during which many other German cities were bombed that it itself might one day be subjected to a comparable bombardment. In this context, it should have expected a massive attack, not only because of its importance as a highly relevant military-strategic transportation hub, but also because of its armament factories and military significance. Dresden was not just a blameless, militarily ignorant cultural city. Its cultural self-determination based on false assumptions, a self-deception, therefore, might also be a reason for perceiving the destruction as a special one and for elevating it to a unique one in its degree of destruction.

On the other hand, what is remarkable in this context, however, is the fact that the attack was aimed less at militarily relevant targets, for example, the barracks complex or strategically important bridges, than at the population and the center of its historically accrued identity. It was not because the bomber force and its strategic initiators wanted to destroy the city's military installations. What made the attack so reprehensible from an ethical point of view and placed it in the light of particularly critical judgment was the intention to bring the population to its knees in terms of its wartime morale. Many of the armaments factories cleverly scattered in residential areas, important railroad connections, and not least the airport with its surrounding military installations were spared for militarily inexplicable reasons. It was all about one goal: to break the population's willingness to go to war and thereby deprive the regime of popular support. It was probably also about more: from personal military-strategic megalomania—Bomber Harris up to the demonstration of superiority and simply revenge. The phrase "like Dresden" may certainly, therefore, also be associated with the fact that the attack lacks the military target that is clear to all. Exactly this also applies to the bombing of Guernica by the Condor Legion in April 1937, which was contrary to international law, and set it apart from the multitude of others: the actual target object of the attack (it was at the center of its justification), a militarily relevant bridge, remained completely intact, but it was a large part of the population and the city that fell victim to the bombing terror under the leadership of Wolfram von Richthofen, who admitted to a "somewhat boorish behavior" of his fighter pilots. Von Richthofen thought the result of the bombing was "just great". It is the scarcely comprehensible discrepancy between military and civilian objects and the focus on the civilian ones that determines the wartime actions of German fighter pilots in Guernica and those of the British and American pilots and rightly casts the attacks on Guernica, as well as those on Dresden, in a special light.

What indisputably contributed to the impression that the attack on Dresden was a special, unique one, and that Dresden could as a result become a synonym for total war, was the firestorm induced by the militarily sophisticated bombardment: A conflagration that ate through everything combustible it can reach, destroying them beyond recognition; a thermal that sucked everything within its reach into the center of the conflagration with indescribable greed; flames that could only finish their destructive work by using all the oxygen they could get their hands on, thus depriving the living creatures within their catchment area, with the result that they died an agonizing death by suffocation. However, the firestorm were also known in other cities, and the most well-known might be that in Hamburg on June 27 and 28, 1943. This was also the work of the allied bomber group of British and Americans, the Bomber Command of RAF and the Eighth Air Force of USAAF. In this context it must be declared—and it cannot be emphasized often enough—that other cities were hit far more seriously in terms of the degree of destruction. What, nevertheless, remains is the shattering experience of the phenomenon of a firestorm and its high number of victims, which is not an everyday occurrence even in the context of war.

Last but not least, the number of victims or, in other words, the assumed number, probably plays a significant role with regard to the fact that Dresden's wartime fate is highlighted from that of other cities to this day. The rather exact and under wartime conditions astonishingly swiftly recorded and documented number of dead—25,000—was quickly increased to 250,000 by simply adding a zero to the originally accurate information and this information was gladly seen and purposefully used by some National Socialist propaganda and spread by other foreign press as quasi-assured. From this point on, this figure, for which there was no true justification, was a self-perpetuating phenomenon that was only later increasingly critically questioned. Furthermore, its momentum continues to have an unbroken effect in right-wing political circles to this day, despite the objective, scientific clarification by a top-class commission of historians. If the number of victims caused by the bombing had been realistically assessed, there might not have been a "like Dresden".

In order to top the list, a parallel to Japan can be made when looking at the ranking that was given to the least fortunate cites in Nazi Germany, as determined by a general assessment, when it is compared to the ranking of those cities that had even endured more destruction under the counterattacks of the Allies. War there is usually associated primarily with Hiroshima and Nagasaki rather than Tokyo, although the loss of life of those from Tokyo exceeded that of Hiroshima and Nagasaki. Hiroshima and Nagasaki attracted the higher attention simply because of the nature of the bomb, the atomic bomb, and the superlative associated with its first use. The suffering and misery of the city of Tokyo paled in the shadow of the atomic bomb being dropped twice. Dresden attracted attention against the background of its former cultural splendor.

Chapter 3

Dresden after World War II

Just as the questions about Dresden before and during World War II could only be answered selectively and by way of example, so, too, can postwar Dresden only be dealt with in excerpts. After a general historical "review" and a war-related "insight", the following peace-theoretical "outlook" in the third chapter is of particular importance. Here—in perspective—impulses are to be taken up which promise an escape from the repetitive vicious cycle of "after the war is before the war", a condition which has lasted far too long in the history of the human race. War, which in terms of intensity and extent rather follows the pattern of a spiral of violence instead of a vicious cycle, can and must—eventually—cease to exist. If Dresden is not a lesson, what kind of inferno it can be?

Biophilia vs. Extermination

Viewed with historical distance and from an anthropological point of view, a war, not only with regard to its course but also its prehistory and its consequences, can only leave the observer perplexed and speechless. This is true all the more so against the background of the countless repetitions of this phenomenon throughout the course of (human) history. If interindividual murderous violence is already incomprehensible, collective violence, as we encounter it in war, is even less comprehensible. Collective violence is so different from what life demands of us day to day in how we cope with it and shape it, that, like a bad dream, we would like to put it behind us and forget it as quickly as possible. Let's just say that we are inclined to suppress it. One essential reason for this may be that, when faced with the magnitude of its appearance, we already resign before the initial attempt to process it. That the evil of war and the indescribable suffering associated with it could occur is more than we can handle. We flee not only from the terribly dark side of life that it represents, but also from the reality which we suspect or know, and with which we are hardly or not at all capable of dealing. A remarkable resilience helps us to let what has come to pass happen and to look forward into the future, and to take its shaping into our own hands on the rubble field of history.

In Walter Kempowski's writings, we read the following with regard to this will for a new beginning, here in view of the reconstruction of Church of Our Lady: "The reconstruction of Church of Our Lady, this undertaking of a defiance of the citizens imbued with love. Anyone who witnesses the care with which it is undertaken, the prudent organization with which what has been destroyed is replaced, and what has been preserved is put in its right place, is moved by the salutary awakening through the rebirth of that which was thought lost." Kempowski even goes so far as to see "the reconstruction of something destroyed" in the context of the phrase "he who sows the wind will reap the whirlwind" and to understand every reconstruction as "a reaction to the sowing of the wind". Even more, and in this he joins the young Goethe, he sees good "ultimately" provoked by evil.

From the same author we can also read and only agree: "We never cease to be amazed at the unconscionability of individuals who push red buttons, and at the courage and drive of others who have to clean up the mess again and again." Alone this observation entitles Kempowski to add yet another book, his own, to the numerous others describing the "hell of Dresden". Others will, he is sure, from "one decade to the next" put the memory of the events in Dresden "into new contexts".

Cities may have been truly "ruined" by major fires like Chicago in 1871 or earthquakes, like San Francisco in 1906, and Tokyo in 1923, by wars, like Warsaw in 1944, Hiroshima in 1945 or other disasters such as floods, tsunami, but also diseases, such as the plague or the recent corona-based pandemic, yet they do not resign themselves to fate and accept devastation. Every tragedy, as Linda Poon sums it up, has a silver lining, however faint. Even if cities have been razed to the ground in large parts, they not only emerge anew after the catastrophe, but often even develop a very special and unique radiance. Thus, through individual as well as through collective traumas, our own biophilic potential drives us with ever new dynamics to lead a life as if its total negation hadn't just occurred. For this irrepressible will to live, simply hinted at here, Dresden is a mighty example. We will take a closer look at this in the following. In the process, different attempts at coping and shaping come into view.

In the aftermath of the Baedeker attacks and the senseless bombing of historically valuable buildings, as well as the destruction, theft and looting of movable cultural property, including sculptures, paintings, books, etc., and in an effort to break free from the vicious cycle of destruction after destruction described here, the international community consequently agreed to *the Hague Convention for the Protection of Cultural Property in the Event of Armed Conflict* of 1954. In this convention signed by 132 states as of 2018, it was agreed to protect certain particularly important cultural property from destruction or misappropriation in the event of war. The objective of the protection agreement is, as it states in its preamble, "that any damage to cultural property, regardless of which nation it belongs to, means damage to the cultural heritage of all mankind". This is justified by the fact that "each people make its contribution to the culture of the world". It is the task of UNESCO to ensure that this is observed. Through the *World Heritage Convention* of 1972, the concern to protect endangered cultural assets is once again confirmed and reaffirmed. The cultural assets worthy of protection are known to all potential belligerents. As far as the Air Force is concerned, they are explicitly excluded from the spectrum of bombing targets. Passers-by recognize their exclusive status, as far as buildings are concerned, by a blue and white emblem [Fig.3-1] visibly attached to the protected structure, usually in the entrance area. The above-mentioned *Hague Convention* of 1954 was preceded by the American Commission for the Protection and Salvage of Artistic and Historic Monuments in War Areas established in 1943 to protect cultural property, and by special units in the British and American forces, such as those of the MFAA (Monuments, Fine Arts, and Archives Section).

Fig.3-1 The emblem of *the Hague Convention for the Protection of Cultural Property in the Event of Armed Conflict* of 1954

Removal of Ruins

What is left for people to do when the war is over? They must first clear away the rubble [Fig.3-2] and mourn and bury the remaining dead. This is always the case. Only after this is done can housing be rebuilt and traffic routes be used again [Fig.3-3]. The reconstruction work done during these periods is immense. Looking forward and the dynamism of the will for a new beginning defy the temptation to resignation and depression. While in the immediate postwar period the survivors collectively and with never imagined energy once again push the engine of civil society, they, nevertheless, also still lack the strength they would need to shape the reconstruction in a demanding or creative way. During this time ruins are thoughtlessly removed without considering the fact that irreplaceable things are thereby forever destroyed. This also happened in postwar Dresden, in some cases long after the end of the war when some of the remaining historically significant buildings were hastily removed.

Against this background, and the fact that the German Democratic Republic suffered notoriously from a shortage of resources (especially material and monetary) until its dissolution, the reconstruction efforts it made—not least in Dresden—deserve special recognition. Here, obviously politically effective, at least partially, it was recognized by certain individuals that what had been destroyed must now be restored and that the necessary material and human resources had to be made available for this purpose—even if it was economically painful (the challenge facing the former GDR is widely documented in books by G. Eckardt).

Fig.3-2 Removal of debris

Fig.3-3 "Rubble railway": light railroad steam locomotive and dump wagons against residential ruins, photo taken after September 17, 1945

In contrast, in the former Soviet occupation zone—for lack of critical awareness of the issues or simply due to economic considerations—much was misconstructed or built over. In terms of architectural history, we encounter prototypes of socialist classicism, such as Stalin Baroque and Stalin Gothic, the so-called Eastern Modernism. Ever since the dissolution of the Eastern Block with the fall of the Berlin Wall and the consequential reunification of Germany with the opening of the Iron Curtain in 1989, it has been a matter of sometimes emotional and fierce discussion, not only in Germany, in how far the buildings and artworks can be subsumed under the genres of Eastern Modernism and, hence, should be protected as monuments and also to which degree they should be preserved in their original state.

Trade also got off the ground quickly, although a lot of improvisation was required. This is what is so amazing: how private entrepreneurship, demand and supply, drove the dynamics of reconstruction and, how in conjunction with employment and earnings along with infrastructural inputs, a new normalization of everyday life occurred [Fig.3-4].

Fig.3-4 First commercial activities to supply the population

Reconstruction

The human will to survive and live becomes evident not least then when she or he, not only as an individual actor, but as a collective, creates a living space that, even and especially under adverse circumstances, allows for survival, according to P. Kropotkin's term of "mutual aid", we can observe the ability and willingness to help one another even in the animal kingdom. With a view to destruction in the context of war in particular, human achievements in construction and reconstruction are especially fascinating. Construction, deconstruction and reconstruction are, as a rule, hardly comparable to one another, especially with respect to time. What requires a long period of planning and execution and is connected with a high expenditure of material as well as personal commitment of construction and reconstruction, can be torn down in a short moment of deconstruction-destruction. The fact that humans, in the face of the fact that deconstruction can never be excluded, or that it has already occurred, and that they build and rebuild even though this might take all their strength, is a remarkable "fascination". This is particularly clear with the example of Dresden. There, (re)construction and destruction have alternated for centuries: for example, during the Thirty Years' War (1618-1648), when Swedish troops burned down parts of Dresden in 1639, or in connection with the destruction of Dresden by Prussian troops in the Seven Years' War (1756-1763), or with the human and material bloodletting in the turmoil of war in the Napoleonic era (end of the 18th century, beginning of the 19th century), and finally with the devastating bombardment towards the end of World War II (1945). Dresden is a master in construction and the reconstruction of its city.

Much of what is destroyed in a few hours remains destroyed forever. The dead cannot be brought back to life, the injured have to live with their debilitations, ideals are eternally lost, many things remain as ruins. Grief and trauma in connection with destruction and death usually dissipate, if at all, only after generations. Dresden is no exception. On the contrary, even 70 years later, the devastating war is still present.

Still, Dresden has rebuilt in the meantime what could be rebuilt. Partly immediately, partly in the course of decades, and this process was in the context and in the periods of two successive political systems: under the conditions of the GDR, former Soviet occupation zone established after World War II, and under the conditions of the reunited Germany, the Federal Republic of Germany, after the removal of the "Iron Curtain". The distinction is not insignificant with regard to an appreciation of the reconstruction effort, because the material and monetary resources available for reconstruction after reunification were different or considerably better. After 1989, which was regrettably late, in some cases too late, significantly more reconstruction could be accomplished than in the years before under the conditions of a consistently weakening economy in the former GDR.

Reconstruction before 1989

The reconstruction of Dresden in former Soviet occupation zone of Germany was difficult on the whole because the necessary financial surplus was chronically not generated, tying the regime's hands as far as investments in restoration work or complete reconstruction measures were concerned. Thus, until the dissolution of the GDR and the reunification of West and East Germany (FRG and GDR) , the initial reconstruction of Dresden's inner city was stringent. In view of the projected high cost of complex reconstruction work, the reconstruction of historically valuable buildings was completely dispensed with in several cases, and the ruins were simply removed—too quickly and often irretrievably.

Initially, Church of Our Lady [Fig.3-5] also fell victim to economic pressure. Here, the regime made a virtue of necessity and decided not to rebuild it, but instead to preserve its ruins as a memorial against the war—the far cheaper, but also not entirely nonsensical solution. In its destructed state, Church of Our Lady (with two side walls protruding from the ruins), according to the declared intention of the GDR leadership at the time, was to motivate people to act for peace. The fact that Church of Our Lady, after its reconstruction in the post-socialist era, was later to function as a "worldwide symbol for peace and reconciliation", follows organically from the GDR's original concept, which wanted its destruction to be understood as a reminder and a warning. In the first two and a half years after its completion alone, it counted five million visitors, the most famous among them being Barack Obama in 2009.

The GDR leadership decided differently in the case of the Semper Opera House. It was immediately rebuilt and returned to its original purpose. That the one is a church and thus a religious object, while the other is an opera house, a secular object, is likely to have played a role in making this decision [Fig.3-6].

Fig.3-5 Church of Our Lady

Fig.3-6 Semper Opera House, interior view, after renovation in April, 2011

This achievement was honored in the GDR with issuance of a corresponding stamp [Fig.3-7].

While the GDR's scope for action in terms of monument preservation was limited, in other aspects it did not allow itself to be left behind by the mainstream of representative modern buildings as far as the international competition for self-expression through architecture is concerned. As such, the Palace of Culture [Fig.3-8], built in 1969 and originally equipped with almost 3,000 seats, initially planned as a high-rise building located in the center of the city, may certainly be counted among those post-modern buildings that are also and especially intended to serve representative purposes.

Fig.3-7 Semper Opera House on a stamp (GDR)

A late appreciation of this undertaking is expressed in the fact that the same Palace of Culture (Kulturpalast, called "Kulti" by the locals) was modernized not long ago, and at the same time not insignificantly remodeled. Today it serves, among other things, as a concert hall for the Dresden Philharmonic Orchestra.

The oversized socialist mural "The Way of the Red Flag" (1969) [Fig.3-9] attached to the Palace of Culture is now—after heated discussions—protected as a cultural monument.

Another representative building—demonstrating socialist innovation and production power—was built in 1972 as one of the first rotundas (circular ground plan, cylinder-like shape) in the former GDR. With interruptions, the 50-meter-wide and 20-meter-high rotunda, designed with nearly 1,000 seats, houses a Round Cinema (Cineplex Rundkino Dresden) to this day [Fig.3-10].

Fig.3-8 Palace of Culture, 1972

Fig.3-9 Mural "The Way of the Red Flag", 1969

Fig.3-10 Round Cinema in Dresden

Reconstruction after 1989

The reconstruction of Dresden after 1989 by no means started from scratch, as the example of the Semper Opera House alone shows. Although many ruins and with them decisive structural puzzle pieces fell victim to the clean-up work in the immediate postwar period, while those of Church of Our Lady, for example, were also removed, they were in contrast stored, so that it was possible to fall back on them under the conditions of an incomparably more favorable financial starting position. On the whole, reconstruction was able to make tremendous progress under the new political and economic conditions after 1989 and had realized projects that would have been unthinkable before. In the context of the remarks on the historic old town and its unique architectural structures, the reconstruction work that took place especially after 1989 has already been acknowledged in detail.

Here, the reconstruction of Church of Our Lady may once again be pointed out as an example [Fig.3-11].

If reconstruction is viewed not only in reference to the historical buildings destroyed during the war, but also in consideration of Dresden itself with the revitalization of the city through new construction projects [Fig.3-12], then a number of remarkable futuristic buildings should be highlighted. These would include the St. Benno Gymnasium (1996), the Crystal Palace (1998) and the Transparent Factory (2002).

Fig.3-11 Church of Our Lady, reconstruction 1996-2006

Fig.3-12 Church of Our Lady after World War II with the reconstructed New Market

Fig.3-13 St. Benno Gymnasium

Founded in 1709 as a Latin school, St. Benno Gymnasium [Fig.3-13] is a state-recognized institution under ecclesiastical sponsorship. As a private school of the diocese of Dresden-Meissen, it bears the name of the patron saint of the diocese, Benno of Meissen. Today, the secondary school is attended by over 700 students. They are taught by more than 70 teachers. The main focus of their education lies in the linguistic, scientific, and artistic areas. The school profile and program place great emphasis on the education of ethical values (including personal growth, social commitment, sociopolitical judgment). The school, which was closed by the National Socialists in 1939, could only be reopened after the dissolution of the GDR in 1990. Since then, it has impressed with its award-winning architecture.

The UFA Cinema Center (Ufa Kristallpalast)—built in 1998 and as a strongly inclined steel and glass construction with a likewise inclined concrete corpus—differentiates itself not only architecturally from the neighboring prefabricated buildings of the GDR era, but also from the round cinema that has dominated the ensemble since its construction. This building—with seating for over 2,500 visitors—is also used for film screenings [Fig.3-14].

When Volkswagen (VW) was planning a manufacturing plant in the center of Dresden and went public with plans for the "Transparent Factory", there was massive opposition regarding the location, since it was proximity to the Grand Garden, therefore would increase traffic volume, bad animal welfare due to oversized glass fronts as death traps for birds and architecturally incompatible with baroque surroundings. Today, the plant which opened in 2002, is in many ways a showpiece of the city and almost a kind of landmark. After varying capacity utilization, VW is now producing its electric car in the "Transparent Factory" [Fig.3-15]. Interested visitors can witness the manufacturing process live.

Fig.3-14 UFA Cinema Center

Fig.3-15 The Transparent Factory (Volkswagen manufacturing plant)

Politicization of a City

Dresden has since recovered from the war, although the scars of its destruction are still strikingly fresh, at least in cultural memory, even after more than 70 years have passed. The fact that the memory remains alive is probably also a positive side effect of the challenge to counter the never-ending legends of lies, especially by the right-wing political camps, with sober truth. As contradictory as it may seem, the attempts of right-wing ideology to appropriate a "destroyed" Dresden against the Allies, especially England, and to stylize Germany as a victim of the war, contribute to the strengthening of memory and significantly to the elaboration of facts on the basis of meticulous investigations and their resilient results.

Through the anthropological and international expansion of the work of reflection (instead of a merely historical as well as nationally narrow one), Dresden's appeal is not solely that of a rekindled "Florence on the Elbe", but also that of a postwar German city which, when reflecting upon its history, has faced and is facing up to the responsibility of being a widely visible memorial to peace. This city was, through all the turmoil of war and war-related misery, and not least through the many disputes about the destruction of its historical core and its victims, allowed to make a tremendous qualitative leap in consciousness. Here, aesthetics has clearly achieved that which constitutes its dignity: namely, to initiate changes in society as a whole through each individual viewer. Dresden now no longer exemplifies—simple-mindedly, beautifully spirited—an intrinsically fascinating baroque or something similar, but also epitomizes, and especially against the beauty of its baroque back-ground, a political consciousness and a corresponding will for change. Dresden is now a reawakened "Florence on the Elbe" and at the same time a widely visible monument to peace. As surprising as its massive destruction, the city has gained an attractiveness and visibility that many cities could only wish for. However, it had not only proverbially, but actually first gone through the fire for this.

According to data by the Dresden Bureau of Tourism from 2017, an estimated of 12 million people (including 30,000 Chinese nationals) visit the city of about 550,000 inhabitants every year, and nearly six million spend the night.

They visit Dresden not only to spend time at the historic Christmas Striezel Market (since 1434 AD) [Fig.3-16], but, above all, to admire the art collections and the aesthetic beauty of the historic buildings and squares, which, although highly regarded, were still torn into deep misery, but regained its splendor anew to then serve as monuments reminding that a "like Dresden" destruction at any cost must be avoided in the future. Today, Dresden is again a beautiful city as much as it is a political one.

Furthermore, Dresden can be described as a green city, as almost two thirds of its considerable area consists of forest and green space. Incidentally, with an extension of about 600 square kilometers, Dresden is the fourth largest major city in Germany in terms of area after Berlin, Hamburg and Cologne. It is no wonder, then, that with these dimensions the Elbe can meander through the city area for over 30 km.

Fig.3-16 Christmas Striezel Market

Dresden, however, is not only a tranquil city of art and culture in the green, but also a development-oriented, ambitious technology location, in fact probably one of the strongest in Germany. Because of its recognized achievements in the electronics sector, Dresden is also called "Silicon Saxony". On the one hand, the city borrows this name from California's Silicon Valley and on the other, the phrase underscores its location in the province of Saxony. Similarly, the term "Florence on the Elbe", linking Dresden's location on the Elbe with Florence in Italy was commonly used for Dresden long before that. In both cases, the associations speak for themselves.

Media, information and communications technology alone employ close to 50,000 people. Among its nine institutes of higher education, the TU (Technical University) Dresden, an elite university since 2012, is best known and with nearly 35,000 students, which is one of the largest in Germany. In the art scene, the Dresden University of Fine Arts is highly reputable. In addition to nearly 50 museums, there are 60 galleries, 80 libraries and archives, 35 theaters and performance venues, 17 cinemas and two orchestras. If you are particularly interested in cultural monuments in general, you will find a network of about 13,000 in Dresden alone. If you have a strong interest in nature, you can find nearly 15 nature and landscape reserves and more than 100 natural monuments in Dresden, according to official information from the city.

As the capital of the state of Saxony, Dresden is also home to the Saxon State Parliament and numerous other authorities. In 2015, the European Council of Ministers awarded Dresden the Europe Prize for great contributions to the idea of being European. Among the numerous city partnerships, those with Coventry (since 1959) and Hangzhou (since 2009) deserve special mention. While Dresden and the former are connected by the common fate of area bombardments, the latter is a partnership with a Chinese city.

Already Goebbels knew to politically instrumentalize the bombing of Dresden as an argument against the British-American military alliance by citing disproportionately high numbers of victims. Later the GDR linked the annual commemoration of the bombing with primarily anti-American propaganda. Members of the NPD (National Democratic Party of Germany) appropriated the terrible result of the bombing of Dresden by applying the word "Holocaust" to the destruction of vast parts of Dresden and in 2005, in order to switch the focus of blame, spoke of a "Bombing Holocaust". However, that's not all. Since 2014 and 2015, because of demonstrations held in Dresden, that are initiated, organized and carried out by an association founded in 2014 against a supposed Islamization of Europe, the city has repeatedly and ingloriously been in the headlines. Under the name PEGIDA (Patriotic Europeans against the Islamization of the West), people with primarily right-wing populist and racist attitudes have joined forces. Their demonstrations contribute significantly to tarnishing the image, especially the international perception of Dresden, a city that is as hospitable as it is politically critical, not to mention decidedly tolerant, cosmopolitan, and international [Fig.3-17].

If attention is now also paid here to the loathsome "Neo-Nazism" movement, then it is not only in order to show an unvarnished reality of Dresden, but also to visibly highlight the challenge which Dresden is consistently as much as it is vehemently prepared to face.

Fig.3-17 PEGIDA demonstration

PEGIDA in Dresden is an undeniable reality. Through the founding of parties on the extreme right wing of the party spectrum, this reality is increasingly forming politically as well. However, it is also becoming more predictable. As a result of the founding of parties such as Alternative for Germany (AfD), and, in some cases, double-digit election results for right-wing populists, for example, the AfD was able to win a shocking 27.5% of the votes in the last Saxon state elections in Dresden in 2019. The confrontation with ethno-nationalistic citizens is no longer left to the counter-demonstrators. On the one hand, the external representation of Dresden from the parliamentary level can start anew. On the other hand, the parliamentary integration of right-wing populist movements with its parliamentary upgrading promotes the emergence of the impression that the party's positions are also socially acceptable.

In the long run, right-wing populism at a lower double-digit level is to be expected throughout Europe. Dresden is no exception. Even though it is marked and burdened by its National Socialist past, a fact that is not readily seen and is, therefore, all too seldom mentioned, it also serves as an opportunity, as a permanent reminder and warning. A small party represented in Dresden's city council, Die PARTEI, a satirical party and primarily symbolic in its politics, has reacted to this right-wing populism. One of its representatives, Max Aschenbach, brought about a resolution based on the assumption of a so-called "Nazi Emergency". This resolution was passed by a 39 to 29 vote, upholding and advancing Dresden's everyday and popular democratic culture against all attempts from the right to undermine it. The international press, such as CNN, on March 11, 2019, has picked up the initiative and spread it worldwide under the headline "German City of Dresden Declares 'Nazi Emergency'". In doing so, it has also taken up the criticism formulated by Aschenbach that the city has not done enough against the right wing of society in recent years.

Dresden, that is to say, the overwhelming majority of the population and with them the representatives in politics, associations, churches, culture, etc., not only remains civically and politically "awake", but also vehemently and increasingly opposes the primarily Islamophobic movement from the right, among other things through counter-demonstrations [Fig.3-18]. In spite of the late formation of the resistance against the right, it is now effective and has contributed to many salutary clarification processes in society. On October 21, 2018, the 4th anniversary of PEGIDA, for example, 10,000 people demonstrated in Dresden for democracy, tolerance and cosmopolitanism under the slogan "Heart instead of Agitation" (Herz statt Hetze), and attended even by the Prime Minister of Saxony, the Vice President, and the Minister of Science.

Fig.3-18 Counter-demonstration "Indivisible"

Conversely, PEGIDA members see their views represented by one particular party—AfD, which is ideologically on the far-right political fringe and which is now represented in German parliaments, consisting of federal and state parliaments. The fact that this party has the largest number of supporters anywhere in Germany in this region (in and around Dresden), out of all places, is reminiscent of dark times. Coincidentally, or not quite coincidentally, it is the region of Saxony in which National Socialism achieved its first brilliant breakthrough. 27.5% of the second votes in the most recent Saxony election, got more votes than in other of the German federal states and, with this frightening result, imposed a heavy burden on civil society.

The sincerity with which Dresden is dealing with the burden of the past and the determination with which the majority of its citizens are resisting the rise of a right-wing movement are—there is no other way to put it—impressive both in terms of its extensiveness and intensity. The founding of numerous cultural associations, countless political actions and religiously and inter-religiously motivated and oriented initiatives reflect the image of a lively, dynamic city in every respect. The fact that this is the case is probably due, in no small part, to the challenges that right-wing political movements in Dresden have brought, and continue to bring with them, as well as the unconditional will that what has characterized and moved this city to this day should not happen again: a war embedded in an indescribable extent of inhumanity, the collective destruction as a result of an unchecked fascist policy.

Peacebuilding Activities and Measures

For a long time, some will say far too long, Dresden kept licking its own wounds. Even if some people—especially on the right wing of society, in their own nationalistic way—still tend to do so today, thereby pursuing above all the objective of shifting the blame for the war onto the "aggressors", in this case, the British and American allies, the majority of the Dresden population has long since understood that the reason for the bombing was basically homegrown, that it was reactive in nature. These Dresdeners have realized the task of pointing out to the world the actual underlying connections behind war, and before the background of the consequences of war, warn against it before it comes to pass. The result of this effort is a colorful conglomerate of initiatives, movements and organizations, which, in summary, is committed to a single, common goal, namely, to make it clear that war should not be there. Positively formulated, one can say that humanity must resolutely seek and realize forms of peaceful coexistence.

The Search for Truth

It took a long time—the annoying provocations from the right and a determined mayor—for Dresden to decide to examine the bombing of Dresden as objectively as possible through the meticulous work of a commission of historians. The Historical Commission on the air raids on Dresden between February 13 and 15, 1945, convened in November

2004 by the mayor of the state capital Dresden, Ingolf Roßberg, was not only to determine as precisely as possible the number of people who fell victim to the bombings, but also to shed light on the events as a whole employing computer tomography. These also include the actual extent of the destruction, i.e. among other things, its spatial extent, the degree of destruction of public buildings and factories, of private apartments and houses, and of the transportation network. Resilient material, that's what the head of Dresden wanted. The mayor wanted to contribute not only to the deemotionalization of the internal social discourse, but also to provide a basis for all further investigations and publications. In fact, it is no longer possible to go back beyond the results of the commission's investigations. They have set standards in many respects. Future research and discussions cannot be conducted without them.

The controversial topics to this day include, in particular, the questions of the will-forming or action-guiding interests of the Allies, the motives of politicians and military leaders, and the ethical evaluation of the bombing, especially the area bombing by the British Royal Air Force.

The investigations have reached a new level of complexity with the scholarly advance of Dietmar Süß. He illuminates and evaluates military operations in the large, factor-rich context of the societies involved in and affected by war, in other words, war society. In this way, he moves away from an evaluation based primarily on quantitative research results, such as individual attacks, weapons systems, bombardments, number of bombings, deaths and injuries, etc. Here, for example, the question of how individual churches behaved toward the war plays a role, among other things.

Motive of the Allied Forces

One of the stereotypical claims, especially of the political right, is that Dresden was attacked and razed to the ground out of the Allies' pure desire to destroy. A "reasonable" military objective, for which there was no reason, is excluded.

In contrast, it is true that Dresden was a potential and likely target for the Allies, both in terms of its industry, in particular its armaments production, and in terms of its militarily strategic significance. From this viewpoint, the bombing of Dresden should have been expected, at the latest ever since the bombing of Leipzig (1943 and 1944). This indeed had been foreseen within certain circles, as the Gauleiter of Dresden had a bunker built under his villa. Nor was the population of Dresden surprised by the extent and intensity of the destructive bombing. It was only because the Gauleiter of the city—in disregard of the Reich air protection measures prescribed by the National Socialist government, and of a previously recognized particular threat to Dresden—chose to invest in immediate war-economic activities instead of investing in air protection, that Dresden was then undersupplied with regard to air protection. That being said, the first bombing raid on Dresden took place on August 24, 1944, a second one on October 7, 1944, and a third on January 16, 1945, before Dresden was hit by the four devastating waves of attacks in February 1945 that were destructive to an extent previously unknown in Dresden, the first of which was on February 13, two more on February 14, and a final one on February 15. The two later bombardments, one on March 2 and the other on April 17, 1945, further underscore the military significance attached to Dresden. Dresden was bombed—clearly not without military calculation—on a total of eight separate dates and, objectively viewed, should have expected to be a target of military counterattacks even earlier.

After all, until the end of the war Dresden was not merely a site where large military formations were stationed. North of the city center, a specific district (Albertstadt) had been established as a self-sufficient military city (with one of the largest contiguous barracks complexes in Germany) already in the 1870s. This area was used and even further expanded during the National Socialist era. In addition, various command centers had been established in Dresden and the Luftwaffe was provided with its own aerial warfare academy and considerable barracks complexes on site. Dresden, which in February 1945 was the last surviving garrison city of the Eastern Front, was bombed—according to a military routine—because, as Frederick Taylor historically accurately and soberly notes, it was highly militarized. In addition, at the beginning of the war, Dresden was one of the largest industrial sites in Germany, and the industrial plants were often located in the middle of, or were installed close to, residential areas. About 50,000 men and women worked in the approximately 110 industrial plants that, by the end of the war, had purely been converted to the production of armaments. In addition to the forced laborers, who were housed in numerous camps spread throughout the city, as well as internees from ten outposts of concentration camps, a few months before the end of the war another 5,000 people, including 2,000 Jewish fellow citizens as well as prisoners, were employed in factories relevant to the war economy.

The fact that the city on the southeastern edge, in a kind of blind spot of what was then Germany, was not attacked until the end of the war can be attributed, among other things, to the distance that Allied aircraft had to cover. In view of the range problem, other targets were simply closer. However, the fact that an attack on Dresden still made inherent sense from the systematic point of view of the military politicians and officers at that time, was due to the fact that Dresden is also an important junction in the traffic network between Berlin and Prague, Leipzig and Warsaw and the troop supply was effectively carried out via Dresden. Alone as a rail hub, Dresden, as the seat of the Reichsbahn division, with its freight and marshalling yard, as well as with repair facilities and railroad depot, was one of the most important transshipment points relevant to the war. With this in mind, the bombing of Dresden was a central concern of the Red Army. The latter agreed with the other Allies on a specific target line and target list for bombardments on the Eastern Front by the Western Allies. Incidentally, had the bombing of Berlin on May 2, 1944 not been possible due to unfavorable weather conditions, Dresden would have been the alternative target and, thus, subject to a massive bombing already on that day, and which would have then been a good year before the actual devastating bombing.

The answer to the question "Why Dresden?" is a very simple one for Sven Felix Kellerhoff: "The baroque city was destroyed because the British Royal Air Force was able to do so." It is, in his view, the "somewhat random" culmination of a bombing war. Just considering their own experience—that the air raids on London in 1940 by the German Luftwaffe did not contribute to the disintegration of the population, but to its cohesion—should have put a big question mark behind the military-strategic or military-political sense of "moral bombing". "Moral bombing" was and is, in military terms, not as successful as Bomber Harris and others would have liked. However, according to Frederick Taylor, the notion that area bombing (such as nighttime attacks against residential areas by the RAF followed by daytime raids by the USAAF) could drive a wedge between the German people and the Nazi elite and defeat Germany had its adherents right up to the end of the war.

The strategy of area bombing on the part of the British, aiming at the demoralization of the population, has at no time been uncontroversial both ethically and under target aspects (not even among military officers), but was, nevertheless, a central strategy and in this respect distinguishable from that of America, who directed at primarily militarily relevant objects. The pragmatic and ethical aspect of this will be taken up again below. Here, it should suffice to point out that with the bombardment, one last bastion of the National Socialist aggressors was to be razed.

Number of Casualties

An ongoing topic of discussion about the bombardment of Dresden's city center is the claim that the number of casualties run into the hundreds of thousands. In extreme cases, without any evidence, the figure of half a million is produced, and even 750,000 dead have been quoted. It is not only the spectrum of the political right, which puts forth gigantic figures, but also that of the political left, even though by now this is in contradiction to any proven knowledge.

While the right-wingers employ unverifiably high counts of casualties in order to whitewash and reverse the role of the perpetrators as victims themselves, the leftists exaggerate the number of victims in order to support the argument that the Allied forces were interested in making sure that the approaching Soviet force and its government find a Dresden destroyed as extensively as possible, thus minimizing the profits of the communist allie as much as possible. Others do not want to exclude the possibility that the Western allies intended the bombing to demonstrate their strength to the Soviet ally before the end of the war.

One of the core arguments for claiming high numbers of victim casualties is that among them are those who are unaccounted for, or no longer could be accounted for, because in some cases, they and their remains were incinerated not only beyond recognition but to the point that there were no remains left. Another argument is that among those to be mourned were a disproportionately large number of, in particular, East Prussian and Silesian (transit) refugees.

In fact, refugees were present in Dresden at the time of the bombing. However, due to a transit regulation, they were only allowed to remain in Dresden for a maximum of one night and were, under any circumstances, banned from settling there. The number of refugees who spent the night in Dresden was, therefore, manageable and limited. Presumptions of a "city of Dresden overcrowded with refugees" do not correspond with reality, but are parts of persistent myths, resisting any rational efforts to correct them. Even in an interview as late as 2015, the military historian Matthias Rogg, who should be familiar with the facts regarding the refugee situation since he referred to the final report of the Historical Commission, still mentioned a city "full of refugees". Against the argument that due to high degrees of combustion, many of the citizens who died in the firestorm were burned without residue and therefore could not have been recorded statistically, the fact that even in the case of a firestorm those temperatures which would lead to corpses burning without any residue, are not reached. For this, as Sven Felix Kellerhoff calculated in one of his numerous worthwhile contributions, temperatures above 2,000 C would have to be attained, but this was never the case, even during the Firestorm. In the case here, temperatures of "only" between 900 C for outdoors and 1,200 C in closed areas were reached. In crematoria, the cremation of corpses requires a combustion temperature of 850 C, for one whole hour, even after which the bones will not have burned and must be ground for burial in an urn.

A counter argument regarding the equally persistent assertion of unrecorded, clandestine burials is the mere fact that there was no apparent reason for secrecy, but also that the clearing of certain areas cited for this had been carried out in the year previous to that of the bombardment and that, incidentally, there was not a single witness for burials of this kind. Last but not least, it begs to question who could have seen any sense in clandestine burials. Certainly not the representatives of the National Socialist regime. They were interested in using references to the consequences of the military attacks from the Allies to unite the population against the enemy.

Other arguments are based on allegations of omitted recovery or incomplete registration of casualties of air raids. The Historical Commission easily refuted all of these lines of argumentation, not least through referring to statistical surveys of the Allied airborne warfare in Germany and its consequences. The mere fact that such figures would be completely beyond the frame of what applies to other German cities in the context of bombings, speaks against the assertion of strikingly high numbers of such victims.

The Report of the Joint Relief 1941-1946 of the International Red Cross puts the figure at 275,000 dead. Today we know that these and comparable figures are based on deliberate false reporting by National Socialist propaganda. As early as in March 1945, for example, the Foreign Office instructed German delegations in neutral foreign countries to proclaim up to 200,000 deaths in their casualty reports. By adding a zero to the (realistic) casualty estimates from back then, wartime propaganda was able to promote a dualism of figures which, as we can see, to some extent, still has its intended effect today. The intension behind the dissemination of exaggerated numbers of casualties, both at home and abroad, as it is with the falsified information about the degree of destruction of buildings, was to portray the Allies as barbarians and discredit them as war criminals. Based on a self-referential system of argumentation, ignoring all scientific evidence is a "tradition of independent publication".

Noteworthy is that the Historical Commission, in the course of its meticulous investigations, could by and large only confirm the numbers of victims had already been officially established a few weeks after the bombings, 18,375 on March 10 and an updated 22,096 three weeks later. Just one week after the bombing, the Dresden police chief estimated 25,000 victims. What stands out as most significant across all calculations are the comparable dimensions in terms of numbers and the absence of claims of detailed accuracy, which should definitely not be understood as indication that any single dead human is more or less significant.

The fact that those citizens who were directly affected by the air raids remember and estimate greater numbers can be explained through their—quite understandable—individual consternation. Here, with all the dignity of personal memory—the commission worked expressly also with autobiographical testimonies and meticulously collected "oral history"—the inaccuracy of narrated depictions must be presumed and they must be critically questioned in detail, regardless of their general permissibility. In this context, a successful collection of more than 50 memoirs is the result of a writing competition organized by the Saxon State Agency for Civic Education.

In response to the thesis put forth by Franz Kurowski, that any quantification or reduction of the numbers of those murdered, gone missing or the wounded amounts to "disregard" and is therefore prohibited, it is the objection that precisely false assumptions and claims and the credulous, or even intentional, acceptance of such represents a disregard of the victims, given that under such circumstances it is not the deaths of individuals which are the dominant objectives. It is indeed the attempt at accurate historical research that honors the actual victims as real victims and does not make them and fictitious others the pawn of ideology-driven argumentation. The ideological orientation of authors, such as Kurowski, is countered above all by attempts to determine the number of victims as objectively as possible and, in this context, inevitably correct the figures that have been circulating in many cases downward. They believe that they can divert attention from Germany's war guilt to one of the Allies by using figures that are as high as possible.

From the standpoint of the theory of science, even seemingly reliable research findings must always be probed anew. The results of the work carried out by the Historical Commission cannot be exempted from this. Therefore, the right to conduct investigations and thereby come to different results cannot be denied. What is note-worthy here is that, almost by rule, the authors of such findings are amateur researchers who, out of the great consternation of their own experience as a child or adolescent, are striving to make the fate of Dresden, through higher numbers of victims, as compared to the figures released by the Dresden police immediately after the bombing, appear even more tragic than it already is. At play is also the inclination towards reversing the perpetrator-victim constellation in such a way that the British and Americans appear as the actual perpetrators or aggressors.

Legends and Myths

What is to be examined in connection with the assertion or ascertainment of victim numbers is also the opposition held by Franz Kurowski against Götz Bergander's claim of a "rabbit hunt" (Hasenjagd). It is one of those—historically groundless—narrative images that serve to maintain a certain world view (directed against the British and Americans) and are repeatedly used in this sense. What is meant is the idea that the Allied bomber units not only bombed the city and strafed residents with on-board weapons, but also deliberately hunted down individual people by low-flying aircraft. Thus, they are said to have been literally pursued and shot by low-flying aircraft as they fled the city—like rabbits being hunted. The fact that both on-board weapon fire and low-flying air raids are unfounded could be conclusively clarified from different perspectives—as we believe—by the Historical Commission appointed by the Dresden city council. As Götz Bergander in 1977 and Helmut Schnatz in 2000 have already pointed out, there was no "low-flying strafing attack". Frederick Taylor also contradicts the claim that low-flying aircraft shot at people. Likewise, the Historical Commission in its final report—based on a broad investigation—dispels the claim of a low-flying air raid. That there could be no order for a low-flying strafing attack is already explained by the context that low-flying aircraft would have made bombing possible for the higher-flying bombers only at the price that they themselves could have been hit by the bombs of their own air force. Even if many may not like it: The often claimed low-flying air raid in Dresden is nothing more than an "urban myth", a symbolic narrative image, however, well suited to condemn the wartime actions of the Anglo-American bomber units as morally particularly reprehensible through the idea of a helpless refugee on the ground on the one hand and a highly armed pilot in the air on the other. According to this historical revisionist assumption, the Allied soldiers bombed Dresden not only from the anonymity given by distance, but even eye to eye, possibly even with pleasure.

In contrast, direct bombardment of citizens can be inferred neither from the operational orders concerning the bombardment nor from reports of pilots.

Individual episodic reports, in which there was talk of shelling on the outskirts of the city, were taken up by Goebbels for propaganda purposes and shifted to the center of the city. This finding is further corroborated by the fact that no such munitions were found during thorough soil sampling in the Elbe valley and that, for various reasons, the pilots would not have been able to carry out the "rabbit hunt" they were accused of.

Degree of Destruction

Christian Bangel brings it to the point when, in his review of the military destruction of Dresden, he speaks of a "challenge". He indicates not only the images of the Dresden firestorm, but also memoirs, such as those of Victor Klemperer, and the countless reports of the mass deaths in Dresden, and also stresses that previously "the Germans had terrorized millions of Europeans" and illustrates this with four selected examples as Guernica, Warsaw, Rotterdam and Coventry. He vehemently opposes the temptation "to see the fate of Dresden as something unique", as something "that stands out among the horrors of World War II", when he states, "It does not. One cannot commemorate the victims of Dresden without naming the Nazis' habitat (Lebensraum) and racial ideology and mourning the many people, especially the Jews, who had been murdered by them by then, without remembering the many other cities of Europe that were destroyed by the Germans". Of course, Klemperer also knows and emphasizes, that the excerpt from the reality of World War II—with respect to his four examples—is "painfully incomplete" and "people have experienced something similar or worse". Accordingly, his summary is clear: "You can see from these four cities: The horror of the nights in which Dresden was bombed originated in Germany." There is nothing more to add to this here.

Ethical Orientation

The strategy of area bombing advocated primarily by the British Royal Air Force, its Area Bombing Directive, which aimed at demoralizing the population and influencing the political and military leadership, accordingly, is highly controversial to this day, both from the point of view of military strategy and ethics (see below) and was so even at the time of the war.

Militarily, area bombardments often achieved exactly the opposite of their actual intention: in the face of indiscriminate destruction of military and civilian objects with sometimes devastating collateral damage, the will to resist and persevere often grew along with the incomprehension and anger of the population. The National Socialist government knew how to use this context again and again for propaganda purposes and to convert the horror about the bombings into approval of its warfare. On the other hand, it also knew that too much emphasis on enemy attacks, such as with phosphorus, could have a demoralizing effect. As a rule, the losses caused by bombardments were not truthfully reported and were downplayed through various media channels. The population allowed itself to be deceived time and again.

White phosphorus munition was used for the first time by the British bomber fleet in an attack on Lubeck during the night of March 28 and 29, 1942, as well as in Hamburg. According to the Historical Commission, it was not used in Dresden. Nevertheless, white phosphorus munition should be briefly mentioned, as it could have increased the destruction of the center of the old city. As a kind of chemical weapon, it should today actually fall under the ABC Weapons Ban of 1949 and be banned from use. This is in view of the possible collateral damage among the civilian population, due to the fact that it is not possible to discriminate between military targets and civilians with white phosphorus munition. As a result, it not only causes "unnecessary injuries" and "pointless suffering", but also causes lasting damage to the environment—further criteria suggesting out-lawing white phosphorus munition. Explicitly, however, even today the United States and Israel do not want to relinquish them. They were used by the Americans in the Iraq War, by the Israelis against Hezbollah. The perfidious thing about white phosphorus munition as a kind of incendiary bomb is that it is highly toxic due to the vapors produced when it burns at about $1,300°C$ and leads to a certain and agonizing death in case of inhalation. Moreover, it causes extreme burns, especially when combined with a rubber mixture that makes it almost impossible to get rid of the phosphorus. The white phosphorus contained in it ignites on mere contact with oxygen and can, therefore, reignite after being extinguished with water.

Sixty years later, British philosopher Anthony Clifford Grayling judges the bombing of Dresden and Hiroshima to have been not only morally unjustifiable, but also, from a military strategic point of view, unnecessary. In his view, the area bombings cannot be called war crimes because at that time the hitherto unknown phenomenon could not yet be classified as such under international law. They are, notwithstanding, "crimes in the moral sense".

Frederick Taylor, also from a British perspective, agrees. For him, the fact that the death of civilians was not only militarily accepted, but also strategically desired, meant that an ethical line had been crossed. Area bombardments, as the British Royal Air Force flew against Dresden, among other cities, were, in his view, not ethically justifiable. After decades of research and a special research project on the bombing war in Europe, Richard Overy had also come to the conclusion that the bombing raids, due to their great degree of destruction and above all to the disproportionately high loss of human life, came at such an excessive high cost that they were neither decisive nor ethically justified. In this context, one of his findings weighs particularly heavily: RAF, in comparison with the other air forces involved in the war, had been the only one to advocate the targeting of civilians in terms of military strategy.

The striking fact that militarily highly relevant facilities were spared or excluded from the bombing, irrespective of any military-strategic consequences, emphasizes that the RAF was conscribed to and virtually fixated on a "moral bombing". The RAF was indeed focused on the civilian population. To cite just one example: The Dresden Pilots' Forge (1935-1945), the Air War School in Klotzsche, i.e. in the immediate vicinity of the Dresden airfield, as well as the airfield itself, were spared from bombardment. This was, in terms of military strategy, an "absurdity", if the omission cannot be traced back to the foresight of utilizing the infrastructure of the airport for future occupation purposes by the Allies. However, if it is true that one ally did not want to give the other too great of an advantage in the conquest of German territory, then the schools for air warfare and the airport should also have been targets of attack.

After his Europe-wide investigations on military history, which were conducted with impressive meticulousness, Richard Overy, along with Dieter Süß, increasingly views war in terms of war-societal circumstances, and no longer only in terms of narrow military-political or military-strategic ones. War research as a whole seems to be in the process of taking a qualitative leap and is far from having reached its full potential. Critical peace research, which is not only dependent on individual studies but also wants to see war described and explained in the context of society as a whole, benefits enormously from the developments initiated so profoundly by Süß and Overy.

In the retrospective ethical assessment of the bombing, the question of who started the "total" war, which was decisively made possible by the Luftwaffe, plays a significant role. According to Franz Kurowski's historical revisionist view, General Trenchard in England and General Douhet in Italy were the first to consider the use of an air force that explicitly included the indiscriminate bombing of the enemy already after World War I. Franz Kurowski, who in his numerous, right-wing populist publications seeks to minimize Germany's responsibility for the war by highlighting the suffering experienced on the German side, associates the view with the strategies designed in this context, that the idea of a bombing war, which was no longer directed at military or war-relevant civilian targets alone, originated with Generals Trenchard and Douhet.

With good reasons, Olaf Groehler can argue the military-historical view that it was Hitler's Germany that put into motion the spiral of area bombing, i.e. the indiscriminate bombing of military and civilian targets. It was Germany which as early as in 1933 considered the use of explosive, incendiary and gas bombs against civilian populations and which in April 1937, during the attack of the "Legion Condor" on Guernica, actually bombed not the military-tactically relevant bridge, but explicitly and across a wide area, the civilian population— with the well-known devastating consequences. This was captured by Pablo Picasso in his universally known mural [Fig.3-19].

Reiner Pommerin takes a differentiated look at the developments from the targeted destruction of military relevant installations and movements to area bombing directed against the civilian population. He sees the attack on the city of London as "Air Scare" at the end of World War I by the German Zeppelins and the so-called giant bombers as the decisive turning point. It was only against the background of its negative experience with strategic bombers—the British had nothing to counter them that the British government concerned itself with general questions of air warfare, and established British Royal Air Force independent of the army and the navy. Already at that time of 1917—in line with its tradition of naval blockades affecting the entire population—Britain envisioned a total bombing war directed against German cities. Thus, the "War Manual", which was essentially coined by General Trenchard, was intended not only to knock down the enemy forces, but also to shake the morale and resistance of the enemy by bombing in such a way that the population would influence the political leadership towards stopping the war actions as "moral bombing". The bombing was intended to bomb some sense into the enemy. There was no longer a distinction between the civilian population and the military, and instead both were understood as two sides of the same coin. Area bombing does not mean that civilian casualties are strategically considered and accepted as collateral damage, but that they are at the center of the strategy. As far as *the Hague Convention for the Protection of Cultural Property in the Event of Armed Conflict* was concerned, the foreboding push by some jurists in 1932 to prohibit aerial bombardment with the aim of terrorizing the population did not succeed. In contrast to the British war strategy, the American one followed the military principle of distinguishing between war-relevant installations and the civilian population and, therefore, to destroy primarily and purposefully military as well as central infrastructural installations.

In historical retrospect, it is easy to look at the bombing of Dresden from the end of World War II and formulate that Dresden was bombed as a matter of course even shortly before it ended. At the moment of the bombing, however, those responsible could not yet think so clearly of an end, even though it could

Fig.3-19 Pablo Picasso: *Guernica*, 1937

be assumed to be near. What in retrospect, from a secure retrospective, can be simply formulated—Dresden was bombed shortly before the end—and, therefore, appears to be particularly reprehensible, is somewhat different at the moment of the event: even if it appears to be the end of the war or not too far from the end, the bombing—viewed immanently from the point of view of military strategy—can be viewed by those responsible for it as purposeful, since the destruction of militarily was relevant as well as moral resources, and justified in terms of military ethics. An ethical assessment of the area bombing in the unquestioned framework of purely military thinking must establish that the Allied military wanted to advance the victory with their action, of which they could not be as sure at the moment of the bombing as the historian in his retrospect. This is not to say that their decision to engage in area bombing and its execution cannot be ethically reprehensible even under these narrow circumstances. Quite a few believe that area bombing, regardless of its questionable timing, as the end of the war is at least looming, was not morally justifiable and cannot be justified in retrospect. From their perspective, area bombing is fundamentally illegitimate.

From another point of view, the proponents of area bombing could see themselves ethically exonerated not only in themselves, but also with regard to a point in time when the end of the war was already in sight. The ethical exoneration of area bombing per se could tie in with the area bombing previously ordered by Hitler: those who themselves carry out area bombings cannot complain about being the victims of it. As far as the ethical assessment of a bombardment that at a certain point in time can only be judged as senseless from the point of view of military strategy is concerned, this would at least be exonerated, again from a system-immanent point of view, by the fact that Hitler himself gave the order on March 19, 1945, to destroy everything during military retreats, when the Western Allies had already crossed the Rhine and the Soviet Allies had already crossed the Oder, that could be of use to the enemy after the capture, for example, from armament plants to transport links to industrial plants of all kinds. Hitler himself, in his own way, so to speak, exposed or wanted to expose not only the enemy but his own population to the fate of a tabula rasa: as an accumulation of the weak and inferior, they did not fit into his Aryan world view alongside the soldiers who had fallen in the war. With them, his delusion of a Thousand-Year Reich could no longer be maintained. However, it was more than just a few, especially industrialists, that had already refused to follow his order for senseless destruction at that time. With regard to an ethical argumentation in the interest of justifying the destructive attack on Dresden, however, the reference to Hitler's Nero order (Nero had had his own city set on fire) should not be irrelevant. He who is ready to destroy the last preserved achievements of his own nation himself must not—actually—be surprised and complain about the destructive work of his enemies.

The same Hitler—with the decline of the Thousand-Year Reich in mind—had six men, his "last captured opponents", hanged still at dawn on April 9, 1945 in the Flossenbürg concentration camp. The theologian Dieter Bonhoeffer, the officers Hans Oster, Wilhelm Canaris and Ludwig Gehre, and the lawyers Karl Sack and Theodor Strünck had attempted to overthrow the National Socialist regime through the assassination of Hitler. On the same night, the artisan carpenter Georg Elser was executed in the concentration camp of Dachau. He had tried to kill Hitler with a bomb in 1939. Also, on the same night, Hans von Dohnanyi, a lawyer, and brother-in-law of Bonhoeffer and co-conspirator against Hitler was executed by hanging. Other opponents of the regime were murdered by SS men in Berlin during the night of April 23, 1945. Johannes Tuchel, "director" of the "German Resistance Memorial Center" in Berlin, sees behind this the regime's intention to persecute its opponents until the last hour, "so that no one could participate in the construction of a new Germany", and as a sign of "revenge", Hitler's "clear and unambiguous desire for and fantasies of final retaliation".

Not least of all, what also should be mentioned—again not in the interest of justifying either area bombing or bombing in general—is that as late as March, with the end of World War II becoming ever more apparent through Germany's surrender, Hitler, as Overy rightly points out, was still flying missions against London. By such actions, of course, those who were ready to hand over combatants and civilians indiscriminately to an area bombardment without remorse see themselves confirmed and purified even after the fact.

From the chorus of those who have discussed and judged the area bombing per se and the area bombing of the British both from the standpoint of military strategy and ethics, the voice of Lothar Fritze shall be singled out for its prudence and perspective as one that makes way for further discussion: "World War II, perhaps the greatest catastrophe in the history of mankind, claimed more than 50 million lives; among them were 25-30 million civilians. The main political and moral responsibility for the European component of this event and its consequences is borne by the National Socialist leadership of Germany. However, it does not follow from this attribution of responsibility that questions about the co-responsibility of the states involved in the war are superfluous. The unimaginable number of victims alone makes it seem necessary to examine the history of this event from the perspective of alternative courses of action. The war of the Allies, especially the fight against National Socialist Germany, is considered today as the prototype of a just war. Both humanitarian interventions and preventive wars have been justified in recent years by invoking the work of the anti-Hitler coalition and the presumed lessons of the struggle against Hitler. This has created a legitimacy resource that can seemingly be easily referred to when needed." Fritze questions an approach of this kind by recalling the "indisputable principle" that "even a justified defender must observe rules in his defense. These rules are partly international law, partly moral". In this sense, he seeks "to demonstrate, using the example of the Western Allied area bombardments of Germany, the burden of justification that must be borne by those who regard Allied warfare as legitimate across the board".

Whether and how absurd bombardments are, in particular area bombardments in the sense of a "moral bombing", or whether they can force a surrender or at least contribute substantially to it, where they could neither in the case of London nor in the case of Berlin, as assumed and represented, for instance, by Bomber Harris and, therefore, are also ethically justifiable, or whether, in the case of area bombing, the use of incendiary bombs against civilian populations constitutes a war crime—all questions of this kind should actually be easy to answer from the point of view of the law of war. According to the United Nations Charter, any war is illegal under international law: "All members shall refrain in their international relations from the threat or use of force against the territorial integrity or political independence of any state, or in any other manner inconsistent with the purposes of the United Nations." That in practice it is different is explained by the long series of exceptions.

The Will to Rebuild and Create

It is as significant as it is astonishing that the people affected by war do not, as a rule, linger long over lamenting their situation but begin to rebuild their destroyed living environment. Their will to rebuild and recreate seems not only not to have been broken by the war, but to have been virtually ignited by it. This will doesn't only lead to short-term responses to destruction, but also manifests itself through later and long-term reactions. These range from (immediate) mere licking of wounds to (long-term) political actions against war and for peace as such. As far as the present publication is concerned, its focus lies precisely in the following description of exactly this will to recreate, in one of its manifold manifestations.

Among the motives for accelerating the reconstruction of a war-torn country, the motive of active suppression is certainly an important one, along with pragmatism. Activism can help to overcome many gloomy memories and the questions that go with them, even if it is only a matter of suppressing the memories.

In addition to large, unspecific segments of the population, the actors include representatives of politics and business, the churches, associations and societies, and other social forces. For professional reasons, academic historians and jurists, explicitly peace scholars, have to deal with the questions surrounding the past war and possible reconciliation processes. In addition to the media, social movements, and educational institutions from kindergarten to university, war and its aftermath are also and especially the subject of art in all its manifestations: from literature and image-based representations to theater and music. If the war itself was not already a field of activity for mediators, the time after it is. Decisions for a war are knowingly made more easily and quickly when compared to successfully finding a way out of war through initiated reconciliation processes.

Professional conflict management in the sense of the search for sustainable peace solutions aims can be broken down into three steps. The first aims at ending a military exchange of blows as quickly as possible through dialogue and non-violent direct action. The second objective is to initiate reconciliation through simply forgiving and even forgetting, up to and including holding truth tribunals. The third step is aimed at bringing about a status between countries worthy of the name "peace". This also includes the exemplary transmission of what has been achieved beyond the concrete areas of conflict between countries to other potential or real areas of conflict that exist between other countries through raising consciousness and awareness on a global scale.

In a time-space diagram [Fig.3-20] with a generous dimensioning of the temporal intervals on the time axis without concrete specifications and a spatial national, international and transnational differentiation, a postwar dynamic can be depicted that neither claims to follow a universally valid norm nor to describe an ideal that is valid for all cases. Regardless of all the specifics of wartime conflicts and subsequent attempts to come to terms with them, a stereotype of coping with war and its aftermath can be gleaned from postwar developments.

In an initial phase, a wartime society, whether emerging from war as "victorious" or as "defeated", is primarily focused on itself and often simply speechless at first. In all cases, human, economic, moral, and many other consequences of war must be addressed locally. The society's perspective is a primarily national one. It is strongly bound by the challenge in its own country, which demands all resources.

In a second phase, the same postwar society broadens its outlook and reflects on the necessity as well as the basic requirements for a new neighborly relationship or peaceful coexistence with the former enemy. It enters or forces them into negotiations. Its perspective is increasingly international. It owes its existence to an increasing openness towards becoming active and the insight that cross-border exchange, dialogue and cooperation have a positive effect on all societies involved.

Postwar activities in a time-space diagram

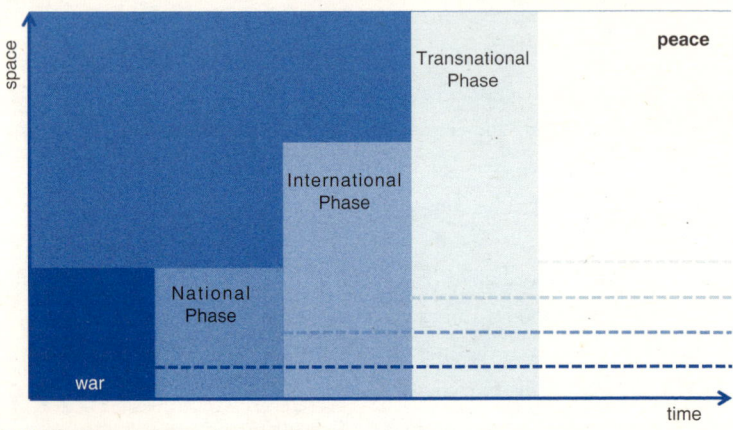

Fig.3-20 Postwar activities in a time-space diagram

In a third phase, the postwar society then uses its status, which is characterized by prosperity and security, not only to stabilize and perpetuate the international network it has developed, but also to make it fruitful for a superordinate, economically and politically binding alliance. Its perspective is now a transnational one. In this way, the society does not give up its special interests, but ideally sees them federally balanced with the interests of the overall network and wider community.

The step-by-step transition from national to international to transnational outlook outlined here is exemplified by Germany's progression after the end of World War II. While Germany was initially preoccupied with itself nationally, it sought and promoted internationally—thanks to an extraordinary and undeserved concession on the part of its immediate neighbors—economic and cultural exchange with France and Poland, among others. Today, the states see themselves united with many others transnationally in the European association of states.

This quite steep development from wartime adversaries to allies by no means signifies the decline of cultural particularities. Instead, it confirms in a hopeful way the view that people beyond their national identities are primarily and quite naturally connected with one another through shared realms of life. On the basis of innumerable universals, all that is needed is a good will to come together and develop a sense of belonging. Where such has been successfully accomplished, everything will depend on not only preserving the status quo of what has already been achieved but also nurturing and creatively developing it.

The progress described here can be strikingly noted by the erection of monuments, for example, in honor of those who died in the war—the first national phase. It can then be traced in the making of bilateral agreements, for instance, in the interest of economic cooperation—the second international phase. Finally, progress will have arrived at its destination at the moment of structural union with a maximum of existential interconnectedness—the third transnational phase. Significantly, the phases do not replace each other. Even with the target phase of transnational connectedness, the two earlier phases—national and international—not only continue to exist, but fulfill their own respective purposes. The cultivation of monuments and the conclusion of bilateral treaties are also in order within a transnational union.

From a slightly different perspective [Fig.3-21], an ascending dynamic could be seen in the fact that a phase of self-pity and egocentric mourning is followed by a phase of asking for forgiveness on the part of the perpetrator of the war and mutual gestures of reconciliation, and this in turn by a phase of efforts not only to interlink in many respects, but even to form alliances or to unite.

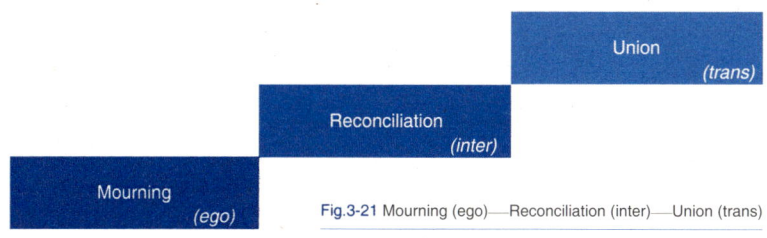

Fig.3-21 Mourning (ego)——Reconciliation (inter)——Union (trans)

Broadening Horizons in Phases

In the case of Dresden, as well, the confrontation with the extensive destruction of its historical core, as well as its industrial plants, military objects, and residential complexes in various city districts, can be roughly divided into three phases—from national self-pity to international reconciliatory action to a transnational commitment to peace. In this context, it is noteworthy that literature and art in the aftermath of the devastating bombing up to the present day—and thus through all phases—have dealt with the inferno or reflect it in their works. National commemoration, international gestures of reconciliation, transnational peace actions paired with never-ending attempts to come to terms with what happened shed light on how deep the wounds of war reach, how difficult they only seem to scar, and how lasting their effect is on those impacted. Before we look at the developments in postwar Dresden in detail against this background, we would like to take a look at Coventry. Not only can the phases mentioned here be traced, but their interconnectedness can also be shown.

After Coventry, with a population of about 320,000 at the time, and as a city important for the armaments industry, among other things, had already been bombed in July and August 1940, on the evening of November 14, 1940, it was heavily hit by the attack of a squadron of 515 bombers, which was cynically referred to as "Moonlight Sonata". Also hit were two hospitals and churches, and last but not least, the St. Michael's Cathedral of Coventry. 568 people lost their lives that night, and more than 1,000 were injured. While the bombing of Coventry, as research confirms, was not specifically aimed only at militarily relevant objects, at least the destruction of housing estates and cultural landmarks was taken into account. It could be that Goebbels made a strategy out of it only afterwards, speaking of "coventration" and thus getting to the heart of the face of the total war terminologically. Others take the likely more accurate view that the strategy of total warfare, with the goal of demoralizing the enemy through high civilian casualties, is depicted in the area bombing at Coventry. After illuminating bombs were used to mark the area to be targeted, 500 tons of demolition bombs and 50 aerial mines to hinder later rescue operations by creating huge craters in the streets and finally 36,000 incendiary bombs were dropped on the city. The devastating bombardment was followed by others in April 1941 and August 1942. Like Dresden in February 13 and 14, Coventry in November 14 and 15 was essentially defenseless against the bombing.

We observe the examples of the fate of both Church of Our Lady and the Coventry Cathedral. The Coventry Cathedral , also known as St. Michael's Cathedral, which had been bombed to ruin, was not rebuilt [Fig.3-22], but rather a new and today extremely popular cathedral was built alongside it, a decision which at the time was met with vehement protest. This is unlike what happened with Church of Our Lady in the case of Dresden, which was "coventrated" by British and US bombers three years later, completely destroying Church of Our Lady in the process. During the GDR regime, it was decided to be preserved as a hortatory ruin in the middle of the city. After the fall of the Berlin Wall decades later, Church of Our Lady was then rebuilt to its almost original state. Both churches became—each in its own right, but also connected by a common fate—a cautionary symbol of the willingness to destroy on the one hand, and the ability and readiness as well as the will to reconcile on the other.

Fig.3-22 Winston Churchill visited the Coventry Cathedral ruins

Even while the mourning community in Coventry was formatting itself after the bombing during the night of November 14 and 15, 1940, the German Luftwaffe flew new attacks on Coventry—following the treacherous strategy of the grueling temporally staggered attacks. To this day, mourning, national commemorations and memorials are present in Coventry. We have therefore assigned the above as the first phase of coping with war and all the associated devastation thereof and assume that it will continue to run through the next phases of coping.

Surprisingly and uncharacteristically early, the second coping phase we refer to approaches the bombardment that must be coped with, and almost overlaps the first one after the latter has just begun. For 40 days after the devastating attack, the provost of Coventry's Anglican parish, Richard Howard, spoke out for reconciliation in a Christmas radio message with these words: "When all this is over, we must reach out to our enemies and build a kinder world with them, in the spirit of Christ the child." "What we want to tell the world is this: Christ has been born again in our hearts today. And as hard as it may be, we banish any thought of revenge." Shortly thereafter, in January 1941, the same pastor had the memorable petition chiseled into the ruins of Coventry Cathedral's "Father Forgive" [Fig.3-23].

Fig.3-23 "Father Forgive"

Notwithstanding the suffering caused by Hitler's Germany and the danger of self-isolation, the Anglican Bishop of Chichester, George Bell, for the first time in 1941 condemned the strategy and practice of area bombing preferred by the British Royal Air Force as morally irresponsible. In addition to him, two members of the Labor Party also opposed it. Winston Churchill may also be mentioned here, who initially ordered the bombing, but later distanced himself from Air Marshal Arthur Harris, who was called "Bomber Harris", and wanted to see the bombing limited—though not for ethical, but obviously for economic considerations: "It seems to me that the moment has come when the question of bombing of German cities simply for the sake of increasing the terror, though under other pretexts, should be reviewed. Otherwise, we shall come into control of an utterly ruined land ..."

Still there were those who must have been deeply affected by the bombing terror of Nazi Germany but, nonetheless, who for moral and economic reasons crossed into enemy territory, even in the time of war, in order to demonstrate international solidarity. This can be seen as an omen, if not realization phenomena of the second phase—concrete reconciliation.

If we can pinpoint a time or a timeframe of when the second phase happened, then impressively early and clearly in the example of Coventry. Already in the early 1950s, the Anglican congregation of Coventry approaches the people of Dresden and makes them an offer of reconciliation. With a time lag, we find the same generous offer afforded in Poland. There, 20 years after the end of the war, the Polish Catholic bishops—against sometimes fierce resistance in their own parishes and dioceses—approach the German Catholic bishops—and remarkably not vice versa—to make them an offer of reconciliation. In both cases, something astonishing happens: not the aggressor approaches the aggrieved, but the aggrieved approach the aggressor; not the terrorist states or its successor asks for forgiveness, but the sufferers of the war, the victims of the National Socialist war policy offer forgiveness to its inflicters and do so. In both circumstances this was the case against sometimes massive resistance among the population. The hand of reconciliation extended to the oppressor by the oppressed is an almost incomprehensible manifestation of unconditional humanity. Not only does such a person have to reckon with massive resistance in his own population, but also has to cope with it in such a way that the offer of reconciliation endures, and the cohesion of the population does not break down over it. For many, the wounds of the war are still all too fresh and the consternation is too deep. For many, the reconciliatory actions of their representatives seem unbefitting, inappropriate and inadequate. For many, they come too soon and are incomprehensible. The acceptance or rejection of offers of reconciliation is often a question of personality: some are more willing to reach out to others and forgive, others find it more difficult. If representatives of church and state do not allow themselves to be thwarted in their willingness to reach out to the perpetrator by those who currently or generally oppose a policy of reconciliation, then they have usually realized that self-pity cultivated in national isolation does not get either side any further and that the one who has the future in mind approaches the other by being able to distinguish between the excesses of a diabolical seizure and exercise of power on the one hand and the people caught up in its undertow on the other. Cross-border reconciliation knows of the dehumanizing effects of a system whose ideology, propaganda and indoctrination people were subjected to or willingly submitted to.

Coventry and Dresden have been partnership cities since 1959. In 1965, young people from Coventry got involved in the reconstruction of the Deaconess Hospital in Dresden, and in 2012 young people from Dresden took part in a youth conference in Coventry. In 2005, with great symbolic power, the Anglican Bishop of Coventry, Christopher Cocksworth, presented the Bishop of the Evangelical Lutheran Church of Saxony, Jochen Bohl, with a cross, which, like the original one first assembled by Cathedral Provost Richard Howard and artistically designed by Professor Geoffrey Clarke, was made from nails found during the removal of rubble from the bombed cathedral. Today, parishes around the world that are committed to reconciliation and peace receive a Cross of Nails from Coventry and henceforth belong to the network of so-called Cross of Nails parishes.

Examples of Coping Strategies

No war is of endless duration. With war a wide trail of destruction is left in its wake, as it is with an avalanche that pushes down into the valley with a great roar. For all its force and violence, sooner or later the structure collapses and a ghostly calm sets in. In both cases, it is the same: those who have survived the catastrophe look overwhelmed, as if petrified, paralyzed, unable to comprehend what has happened, let alone put it into words. War leaves one speechless. Even once the survivors and witnesses from near and far have regained their composure, they are still far from being able to reflect on and comprehend what happened in a larger context. They are concentrated on the event as such and stand before it like the visitor of an extinct volcano at the edge of its crater. They mourn and look for ways to express this mourning, so they create monuments, war memorials, through which and in whose places they commemorate the dead, and they record the events of the war in museums. The reappraisal of the inconceivably terrible begins, and it begins from a point of view characterized by a limited national perspective. It is the same point of view from which the war (whether from the position of attack or from the position of defense) was fought. None of the parties involved in the war have thus far succeeded in shedding their position overnight even after its ending.

Finally, what further inhibits those afflicted by war and those who witnessed it are the limitations in emotional resources and in the capacity to take action. What is still lacking at this early stage is any scope for comprehension, for initiating dialogue, for any kind of reconciliatory action. In other words, that which we would assign to a second phase of war resolution. Here, it is the same as with prosocial behavior: where there is stress and the need to solve personal problems under its conditions, there is a lack of the power indispensable for prosocial behavior. The focus on one's own misery does not permit action that moves constructively toward a transnational and international processing of or a coming to terms with the war.

A processing of the past war from a transnational perspective is not possible at this point. A view of the war from a sober, metaphysically detached level is still a long way off, for this presupposes the luxury of an economically as well as morally balanced society. Let's illustrate this through a parallel recourse: altruistic action, an enhancement of the merely prosocial, presupposes an optimal scope of action in every respect. Without this, it would be bottomless and adventurous. Another parallel: do-gooders in the good sense not infrequently create their social alternatives from the secure position of an affluent parental home. If they had to live from hand to mouth, they would lack the strength and freedom to think beyond the day and to reflect on life in larger social spaces, let alone make corresponding attempts at the realization thereof. The same applies— incidentally—to our ecological behavior: it cannot be responsibly expected from those who struggle daily for their survival. It is demanded primarily from those who have the corresponding economic and intellectual freedom.

The development from national, to international, finally transnational processing of past war proceeds in more or less overlapping phases. This does not mean, however, that where war management moves on a transnational level, the purely national or merely international ones have lost their significance. Each manifestation of war management has its purpose as long as it does not exclude any of the other phases. The memorial in the center of a city, international city partnerships, or a work of art tabooing war by principal and designing an artwork promoting global peace—they all have their purpose and justification. Examples of this in the case Dresden will be discussed below. The assignment to the individual phases is not always unambiguous and free of doubt.

National Commemoration

When one remembers the removal of war debris in Dresden and in this context erects a memorial for the Rubble Women (1952), then one commemorates a war as an experience specifically affecting one's own city. This is done against the background of self-pity, lamentation and accusation, less with a view to the great synthetic connection of doing and being done, of far greater destruction by Nazi Germany in the countries affected by the war on the one hand, for example, one only has to think of Warsaw or Stalingrad, and the consequences of the war on the other of those who are responsible for it. Those responsible also carry responsibility for their cities and countryside, which are above all significant in terms of military strategy and tactics. In this phase of confrontation with the destruction of its own country and city, "Florence on the Elbe" sees itself in particular as the victim of an unjust military action of area bombardment. The fact that it suffers, that it must and wants to give expression to this suffering—regardless of its perpetration—cannot be denied nor faulted but must be granted, without exception, beyond all times. Accordingly, war memorials are also to be seen and understood and also to be accepted and appreciated. Even the aggressor is entitled to and must be allowed to mourn and to express his mourning.

Mourning Service

Faced with the crushing experience of his church being completely burned out (although not collapsing) as a result of the bombing [Fig.3-24], its cantor, Paul Mausberger, fled to his homeland, the Erzgebirge (mountain range between the German and Czech Republic)—under the impression of the hopeless chaos of his city—in order to process his deeply felt grief in a rousing motet. It is Good Friday, March 30, 1945, and Holy Saturday, March 31, 1945, and only six weeks have passed since Dresden had experienced the most terrible of its bombardments, when Mausberger is inspired to compose a moving a cappella piece. He composed "How Lies the City so Desolate" (Wie liegt die Stadt so wüst), taking excerpts from the lamentations of the prophet Jeremiah in the translation by Martin Luther:

How lies the city so desolate, which was full of people. (Jeremiah 1:1)
All its gates stand desolate. (1:4)

How the stones of the sanctuary
lie scattered before it in all the streets. (4:1)
He hath sent a fire from on high
into my bones, and hath caused it to prevail. (1:13)

Is this the city of which it is said,
it is the most beautiful, to which
all the land rejoices. (2:15)

She would not have thought
that it would go like this for her at last; (1:9)
she is indeed too horribly pushed down
and has no one to comfort her. (1:9)

Therefore, our heart is grieved
and our eyes are darkened. (5:17)
Why wilt thou so utterly forget us,
and so utterly forsake us for life! (5:20)

Bring us again, O Lord, unto thee,
that we may come home again! (5:21)
Renew our days as of old. (5:21)
Oh Lord, behold my misery! (1:9)

Fig.3-24 Concert of the Dresden Chorus in the burned-out Cross Church

As in the end the above-mentioned disciples of Emmaus—after making a loop and hastily fleeing the city of Jerusalem, wandering about in the "chaos of feelings", increasing insight into the connections and a lasting realization, which was the image of a surprising meeting with those killed in the context and moment of a common meal)—return to Jerusalem, so also Mauersberger returns to Dresden and to the Cross Chunch. On August 4, 1945, three months after the end of the war, his mourning motet was premiered in the church, which had not yet been restored. Dresden mourned.

Fig.3-25 Rubble women clearing bricks in the ruins of the Exhibition Palace of Dresden

Fig.3-26 "Rubble Women" Memorial

"Rubble Women" Memorial

Because many men had been deployed militarily during World War II and there was—understandably—a lack of men fit for work after the end of the war, numerous women are said to have been deployed for the immediate removal of debris after bombardments or after the war had ended for the large-scale removal of rubble from destroyed settlements [Fig.3-25].

Among them were women who were obliged to remove debris by the occupying forces, but also volunteers. Their work was honored by awards and commemorative days, as well as by the erection of honorary memorials in many cities in Germany, but also glorified in the interest of counterbalancing the Nazi atrocities.

In Dresden, too, the work of the rubble women was honored by a monument [Fig.3-26]. They are said to have been instrumental in the removal of rubble from over 80,000 homes. Such monument was made of cast iron by Walter Reinhold in 1952.

War Memorials

War memorials—we find them in all cities and larger towns, in the entrance and centers of cemeteries, at crossroads and in quiet corners of a city [Fig.3-27]. With short texts carved into them and lists of soldiers killed in the war, behind each name there is a distinct fate: an individual. War memorials, like cemeteries of honor, are often sites where commemorative and mourning ceremonies are held at annual intervals and the dead are remembered collectively, such as wreath-laying ceremonies, speeches, devotions. As a rule, they are commemorated as mere victims. Their deaths are not reflected in the larger war-political contexts.

In Dresden and its immediate periphery, we find today more than one hundred war memorials, among them numerous monumental ones in memory of fallen soldiers of World War I, and some even in memory of the war heroes of previous wars. Many are dedicated to the dead of World War

Fig.3-27 War memorial of the town of Lohne with the inscription: "Dedicated to our brave sons from the glorious campaign 1870-1871. The grateful community of Lohne"

II, not only to individual soldiers, but also to civilians. In some cases, it is the grave of one person, but most are memorials made of stone, metal or wood for several. Several thousand can be found throughout Germany [Fig.3-28]. The American-based online project "Memorials to the Fallen" (Gefallenendenkmäler) successively lists the memorials reported to it and makes the listing, combined with pictures, the text of inscriptions and commentary, generally accessible on the Internet. And the list, already as long as a book, is still increasing in size. The number of unreported war memorials is probably even higher.

No question, the war memorials all reflect first of all the view on one's own nation and its "own" fallen soldiers or killed civilians. Some are characterized by a gaze that is unique to them and their fate. Others also include the other side through the texts on them as they contain the formulation of a reconciliation perspective. As such, one can find boundless memorials which indicate an eschatological shift towards global peace.

A special war memorial, which we find (not only) in Dresden, should be pointed out here: the Soviet War Memorial, which originated in 1945 and today is under monument protection [Fig.3-29]. It is expressly for the "others"—for those soldiers of the Red Army who died in World War II and gave their lives in the Allied war against Hitler.

If national commemoration inevitably must take place on foreign territory, then a linkage of national commemoration with international references will inevitably follow. As such, whole stretches of land are littered with graves of identified and unidentified soldiers of the former German Wehrmacht, as well as civilian war victims in more than just a few European countries considered former "enemy territory" in which they had fallen or were killed. An initiative was founded by the association "German War Graves Commission" (Volksbund Deutscher Kriegsgräberfürsorge) as early as 1919, which combines the care of war grave sites abroad with awareness work and with the aim of contributing to international understanding. The association looks after the graves of 2.7 million war dead in 832 cemeteries in 46 countries.

Fig.3-28 War memorial of the city of Vechta with the inscription on the front: "1914-1918 The fight and death of the brave shall be unforgotten. 1939-1945"

Fig.3-29 Soviet War Memorial in Dresden

Inversely, large cemeteries can be found in Germany where soldiers of the Allied troops as well as soldiers of other formations and also civilians (for example, forced laborers), have found their final resting place. The Soviet Garrison Cemetery [Fig.3-30] located in Dresden, one of the largest of its kind in Europe, was established as a Red Army war gravesite in May 1945. Its management and maintenance have been the responsibility of the city of Dresden since 2019. It is located in the forest and covers an area of 2.3 hectares.

In the middle of a forest, in the middle of a natural landscape, one can again suddenly come across a memorial stone in Dinklage Germany [Fig.3-31], which draws attention to the shooting down or crash of a British fighter pilot at this location. Even in the context of monument preservation, mourning work can have cross-border components and be internationally oriented. Whoever passes the memorial stone will not associate the dead with the idea of an attack but instead with that of liberation.

For many Germans, by the way, redemption from the war took far too long. It is obvious that it could be commemorated in the future with its own—newly introduced—holiday, namely every year on May 8. The Holocaust survivor and chairwoman of the Auschwitz Committee in Germany, Esther Bejarano, demands this and receives much approval for this idea.

An impressive Christian war memorial stands in Bakum, Lower Saxony, in front of a church square. Preceding the classical war memorial with the usual names of the fallen in that place where they lost their lives, a monument with two steles, which is clearly of recent date, reflects the concept of war with the perspective of peace. The stele on the left [Fig.3-32] has the following inscription: "Hatred, hardship, misery, destruction and death, such is war." and, in contrast, the one on the right [Fig.3-33] carries the inscription: "Growth in harmony, blossoming, being fruitful, living, such is peace." Here, a remarkable anthropological arc of tension is established, and war is looked back upon from a great distance.

Fig.3-30 Soviet Garrison Cemetery in Dresden

Fig.3-31 The Memorial in the Town of Dinklage

Fig.3-32 The monumental stele in Municipality of Bakum, the left column

Fig.3-33 The monumental stele in Municipality of Bakum, the right column

In the place, exemplary juxtaposition, the progression of remembering—as a possibility and as a reality—is obvious [Fig.3-34]: the view of the war expressed in Monument 1 is a heroic, national one; that in Monument 2 includes all those involved in the war; that in Monument 3 is a cosmopolitan, transnational one, anthropologically reflective and principled. To use the now familiar term for the third type of remembrance: here, remembrance is enduring and perspectival.

From heroes-oriented to peace-oriented remembering

Monument 1: national perspective

Monument 2: international perspective

Monument 3: transnational perspective

Fig.3-34 "Progressive remembering" (a model from examples)

Fig.3-35 Reminder of the burning of 6,865 dead bodies in 1945

Back in Dresden: A similar action, as done with the "Stumbling Blocks" [Fig.3-35], is depicted in the adjacent picture of a street pavement. There it says on cast-in metal: "After the air raids of February 13 and 14, 1945, on Dresden, the dead bodies of 6,865 people were burned at this site." Of course, it is up to each passerby whether they, bent over the scarce information, stand frozen over the incomprehensible fact of the high number of bombing victims and consider and condemn the bombing as directed against their own nation. Or perhaps they might understand this in the grand scheme of a war event for which their own nation is responsible and then draw from it the admonition to undertake everything conceivable against any kind of war wherever they may take place and to work toward peace.

In memory of the victims of National Socialism, on the initiative of the "Stumbling Blocks for Dresden e.V. (registered association)", founded in 2009, approximately 200 "stumbling blocks" [Fig.3-36] have been set in Dresden to date, the first five on November 4, 2009. Across Europe, there are now more than 75,000. These are a type of paving stone, which has a special surface made of brass and is arranged individually or in groups between the other paving stones or sidewalk slabs or is embedded in other road surfaces. On the surface of each paving stone is engraved the name of a family or a person who was persecuted or expelled because of their Jewish creed, political beliefs, sexual preference, illness, ethnicity, or for other reasons was killed in concentration camps or escaped. As a rule, the "Stumbling Blocks" are inserted into paths or streets where the deported persons last lived. The "Stumbling Blocks" campaign, one of the world's largest decentralized commemorative projects, was initiated in 1992 by artist Gunter Demnig with the laying of the first Stumbling Block in Cologne. In the meantime, more than 70,000 stones have been laid in 1,265 German communities and in 24 European countries. The cost of a stone is about 120 euros and research on the person engraved in the metal plate is borne in each case by a sponsor. In the case of willfully destroyed or removed stones, the procurement of a replacement is resorted to through donations. For Dresden, a consistently updated list of persons to whom a Stumbling Block has been dedicated can be found on the Internet, as well as a map on which the individual stones are located.

Fig.3-36 Stumbling Blocks in Dresden

Reconstruction

The list of priorities regarding the reconstruction of destroyed buildings after the end of a war is understandably headed by those serving housing and transportation, as well as social and educational facilities. The restoration or reconstruction of cultural buildings, including religious ones, is secondary in this phase. This fate was shared by the Semper Opera House, Church of Our Lady and the Synagogue, among others.

There is no question that coming to terms with the past and reconstruction in Dresden includes the remembrance of the Holocaust and, therefore, also the history of suffering of Jewish citizens in Dresden, as well as the reconstruction of the Synagogue [Fig.3-37] destroyed during the Jewish pogrom. Hitler's seizure of power, the Holocaust, and the beginning of the war are to be seen together, especially in view of the obvious experience of the bombing of Dresden, which actually happened late in time from a military strategy perspective.

The reconstruction of the Synagogue [Fig.3-38], of course at its original location, is one of the spectacular achievements of Dresden. This has obviously succeeded so convincingly well that the Synagogue was awarded the title of European Building of 2001 because of its special architecture. Even if others may see it differently, the personal opinion is permitted here that the Synagogue breaks up the baroque Dresden precisely through its monumentally bulky architecture. Through its appearance it catches the eye and makes the intended statement of the "bulkiness" of the Jewish pogrom in all respects. Just as there is actually no room between the baroque architecture for the sobriety of a more or less pure cube, there is no room for the inhumanity of the persecution of the Jews in the midst of humanity.

Fig.3-37 Old Dresden Synagogue by Gottfried Semper

Military History Museum of the German Armed Forces

In general, one expects from a museum dedicated to the military and its history that it tries to depict this through the uncritical, contextless stringing together of individual wars and, moreover, that it operates a kind of weapons show. Military museums are usually regarded as repositories of battles fought, of military strategy, weapons technology, military exhibitions and parades, of soldiers' portraits and biographies. Somewhat exaggeratedly, these kinds of museums could be described as the focus of national self-reflection. We can find them in almost unlimited numbers in every corner of the world, both government-run and privately-owned, especially by war veterans.

Fig.3-38 The new Synagogue in Dresden

Fig.3-39 Military History Museum, Dresden

The Dresden Military History Museum [Fig.3-39] in its present form has nothing in common with such museums. It is not just a museum of the eternal yesterday; it is not just a museum which serves the glorification of war and even its frequent subsequent glorification. It is a museum dedicated to the sober interdisciplinary study of peace and war, especially with regard to their anthropological and historical preconditions or conditions. The museum, with its 10,000 square meters of exhibition space as one of the most important history museums in Europe, presents its permanent exhibition on its website by stating "The focus is on man and the question of the causes and consequences of war and violence". The museum, which has been architecturally modified in an impressive way by star architect Daniel Libeskind, is, of course, aware of its

eventful military history. In 1961, it was still known as the German Army Museum, from 1972 as the Army Museum of the GDR, and even after the takeover by the German Armed Forces in 1990 until 2003, it was still very much characterized by the conventional style of military history museums. It is not only the history of this museum that allows us to study how perspectives can be developed. The positioning committed to one's own nation can certainly give way to an intellectual breadth that takes in international contexts and thus gives way then to the peace education potential inherent in military history.

Forum ERINNERN GESTALTEN Dresden

The Forum ERINNERN GESTALTEN Dresden (REMEMBERING SHAPING Dresden) sees itself as a civic initiative open to all who share the concern of a future-oriented remembrance of Dresden's past within the framework of an encounter committed to democracy, peace and human rights, and who understand the diversity of the city's cultures of remembrance and commemoration as a "productive resource for joint work on the present and the future". The forum supports, among other things, lectures and exhibitions.

As an example of one of the experiences to be found in a special digital memory map of Dresden, let us quote that of Karl-Wilhelm Schubert from Dresden:

> *My personal place of remembrance is the driveway to the Blue Wonder in landward direction. During the action "Swords to Plowshares" I wore the patch on my jacket, which had caused me no problems at work.*
>
> *On my way home after work by motorcycle, I was asked by the traffic policeman at the intersection to park my motorcycle and wait for him. He then asked me to remove the patch. When I refused, he ordered me to wait until a patrol car came to drive me to the station. This at least gave me time to briefly inform my wife. I was then driven to the police station in Leuben, where the officer on duty again asked me to remove the patch, otherwise I would have to stay there overnight. However, I did not want to go that far, but I told the officer on duty to remove it. To do this, he went into the next room, while I used the time to take a rose from the bouquet of flowers intended for my wife and wedge it between two tables. The policeman was very irritated at first and asked what that was all about. When I explained to him that I wanted this to be understood as a sign that I had no personal grudge against him, he was obviously able to accept this, blushing slightly. So we parted quite peacefully.*

International Understanding

When—as the title of this chapter makes clear—we speak here of an international phase with a view to the Dresden "afterwards" and before that of a national phase, this is intended to indicate progress. The phenomena that are classified into the phases and thus distinguished are not always so clearly assignable.

A Children's Book for Reconciliation and Peace (Ferdinand Angel, 1998)

When the impact and success of activities are evaluated solely on the basis of their radius or the amount of funds used, it is easy to overlook the fact that it is often the small, inconspicuous contributions that move a project forward. In the end, it was the countless small donations that made it possible to rebuild Church of Our Lady, among other things.

In this sense, an exemplary reference is made here to a project that arose on the initiative and from a seminar of the religious educator Ferdinand Angel, formerly a professor at the Technical University of Dresden, now at the University of Graz in Austria. His students created a children's book entitled *Adventure in Church of Our Lady* (*Abenteuer Frauenkirche*) out of a seminar course [Fig.3-40]. Intention and content of the booklet: During the one week that the girl Katrin visits her grandmother in Dresden, she comes into contact with the reconstruction of Church of Our Lady in an exciting way. Above all, Paul, an organ grinder, introduces her to the history of Church of Our Lady. Because the booklet—a large part of its proceeds go

Fig.3-40 The cover of children's book: *Adventure in Church of Our Lady*

to Church of Our Lady, is intended to serve Church of Our Lady as a symbol of reconciliation and peace, it also makes reference to Coventry Cathedral and thus, just as obviously and rightly, directs the perspective to the larger international context.

White Roses (Weisse Rosen), Nora Lang, 2005

February 13, 2005 marks the 60th anniversary of the air raids on Dresden. To protect the commemoration day against right-wing extremist instrumentalization and to position themselves against racism, war and violence, thousands of its citizens wear a white rose [Fig.3-41]. The small white roses made of silk are a reference to the "White Rose" resistance group of the same name during the Third Reich. In addition to numerous organizations, the action is supported by the regional press.

The action was initiated by Nora Lang, who survived the bombing as a thirteen-year-old at the time. For over twenty years, the world's most respected peace activist has been working to combat forgetting by telling young people in particular about her own experiences and raising awareness of the issue of war itself. After the attack she had found two porcelain plates—one painted with a red rose, the other with a white rose. Unlike the one with the red rose, the one with the white rose was not touched by the fire. In 2001, as a survivor of the Dresden Inferno, she presented one of the two plates to survivors from Guernica, a city destroyed by the German air force in 1937. Before 1995 she had already initiated the first public meeting in Dresden for the generation of contemporary witnesses of the year 1945. As co-founder of the interest group "February 13, 1945", she writes that whenever she speaks as a survivor of the bombings, it is not about lamenting that her home and parts of her childhood and youth were taken away from her, but "that it is extremely necessary to derive action for peace, for tolerance, for humanity from these painful experiences", emphasizing that like her, "many people in the world have gone through similar suffering due to war, violence and terror and still suffer it today".

As part of the "Peace Heroes" project, her association organized meetings of students from Madrid, Budapest, Sarajevo and Dresden. For two days, the young people explored the history of the city in workshops and asked themselves the questions: What is peace anyway? Who is a hero or where have we shown courage before? They finally presented the result of their discussions to a wide audience in a stage performance on the anniversary of the bombing, February 13, 2018.

Fig.3-41 Symbol: White Rose

Transnational Perspectives

In a third phase (this too is difficult to grasp in terms of time and overlaps with the preceding ones), the city and those who feel connected to it, or are concerned with its destruction due to the war, reflect on the war event holistically. Their reflections are, for example, in the context of the aggressive National Socialist policy and Hitler's war drive and, hence, as a consequence of their own destructive actions. Furthermore, they also take into consideration an action for peace which is oriented towards international or cosmopolitan thinking and which, on the basis of Dresden's specific experiences, is concerned with a fundamental understanding of peace and, connected with this, with learning about peace across nations and cultures. Dresden has become an opportunity and an example for peacebuilding activities directed against war and its preparations "per se". Dresden is home to countless initiatives that are not only reactions to the suffering inflicted by the air raids and the admission of Germany's war guilt, but also correspond to the special task of turning the experience of regret and confession of guilt into transnational peace action. In the following, some will be presented as examples for the many.

Dresden's Splendor and Inferno in Panoramic Art (Yadegar Asisi, 2015)

The panoramic artist Yadegar Asisi, was born in Vienna in 1955, grew up in Saxony and, after studying art in Dresden, now lives in Berlin. On the basis of photographic and textual documents and the numbers of victims determined by the Historical Commission, he created a monumental 360° panorama in 2015 which, combined with an impressive light simulation and musically underpinned by a contribution by Eric Babak, has since been displayed in the Dresden Panorama Museum [Fig.3-42] under the title *Dresden 1945—Tragedy and Hope of a European City* on an area of 3,000 m². From a 15-meter-high platform, visitors look into a 27-meter-high representation of Dresden from the past.

Fig.3-42 Outside view of Dresden Panorama Museum

Remarkably, the artist's sensational circular painting not only expands the view spatially beyond Dresden [Fig.3-43] to Europe, which is drawn as parallels to destruction in Rotterdam, Coventry, Stalingrad and Warsaw, but also directs it temporally from the past into the future, from the perception of a horrific tragedy of war to a hope beyond war.

Fig.3-43 View of Dresden in its destroyed state

Fig.3-44 Visitors on the platform experiencing the panorama *Dresden in the Baroque*

In support of his forward-looking perspective and the credibility of his optimistic view, Asisi looks back to a time of prosperity in Dresden and creates—as a contrast to the harrowing war scene—a panorama of the beautiful, carefree life in the magnificent Baroque residential city between 1695 and 1760. The baroque panorama *Dresden in the Baroque—Myth of the Saxon Residence City* [Fig.3-44], shown at the same location, the Panorama Museum and there since 2015 in periodic alternation with the war panorama, overlays the darkness of the war and substantiates the hope already articulated in the context of the war panorama. Two parrots that were able to escape their aviary in the Dresden Zoo in the course of the bombing and now—instead of the bombers—fly over the destroyed area, perhaps as an allegory to the dove returning to Noah's Arc or of the inconspicuous plant in the severed arm in the war painting *Guernica* created by Picasso. When everything seems destroyed, it is nature that builds a bridge to the future.

Dresden for All

Prewar Dresden already gave space to National Socialism to a greater extent than most other cities in Germany. This is an old debt of the city. Its citizens are still working it off today. And as if the past were not already a burden enough, it even seems to be repeating itself, at least to some extent: in the emergence of a comparatively strong political right wing, all the way to sometimes appalling mergers and actions by right-wing extremists. Dresden's significant right-wing bias is an agonizing nuisance to the majority of its citizens, not least the city's political decision-makers. Even though the lamented right wing is a manageable movement, the external impact of its activities is considerable.

Loudness and rumbling of the right-wing activists contribute to the distortion of the situation to an undue extent. In reality, Dresden is nor a city of the right and certainly neither a right-wing city. Quite the contrary. To demonstrate this, many of its citizens are taking position, launching initiatives and founding associations, and thus standing in opposition to the right-wing mob and its denigration of the city, with a Dresden committed to the democratic spirit. In the context of this confrontation, the way the past is dealt with plays a central role: while some, following a nationalistic attitude and a revisionist view of the world, try to minimize not only the guilt of war but also all the other inhumanities of Hitler's Germany, others stand by Dresden's guilt and accept a connection between it and the suffering that also fell on Dresden at the end of World War II as a result of the well-known bomb inferno. Coping with the experience of war and coping with the National Socialist past cannot be separated, especially in Dresden. Their connection becomes apparent once again in the confrontation of its citizens with right-wing groups. In essence, this is reflected in virtually all cultural activities—only a selection of which can be presented in this publication. Furthermore, this is always in the foreground: unity in consideration of diversity with the exclusion of right-wing patterns of thought and action, as well as the stereotypical invitation to participate in the processes of unification that are reflected in numerous initiatives and associations.

One can already gather a lot from the adjacent, expressive logo and the symbols used in it [Fig.3-45]. "Dresden for All" is, according to the Alliance, "a network of more than 100 Dresden initiatives, organizations, associations and institutions". As such, it advocates a "democratic urban society in which the participation of all is possible", defends human rights and the Basic Law and "against any form of discrimination".

Fig.3-45 Logo: "Dresden for all" (Dresden für alle)

To get an impression of the orientation and diversity of local initiatives in Dresden, which—against the background of the Anglo-American air raids on Dresden, but also and especially of Germany's war guilt—urge reconciliation and peace, resistance against hatred and violence, and non-violent conflict resolution, the following exemplary links should suffice. Their evaluation in individual cases would not only complement the description of the activities mentioned above, but also introduce others and inspire them with regard to their own activities. In terms of diversity and number alone, it makes sense to keep the Alliance in mind.

Currently, the Alliance has supported a variety of projects to date. Among many others:

· a political and artistic education project for adults and young people

· the "Monday Café" in the Little House (Kleines Haus) of the State Theater Ensemble (Staatsschauspiel) as an open meeting place for Dresden citizens and refugees

· an international soccer tournament of the German Lessons for Refugees

· courses by asylum seekers, migrants, and people entitled to asylum in the interest of intercultural exchange

· the Refugees Truck on Christopher Street Day, through which refugees wanted to draw attention to the oppressive conditions in their home countries

· the Kurdish Film Days in Dresden

· a policy forum on the situation of Syria

Dresden. Respect (Dresden. Respekt)

In 2016, with respect to the recognition of the inviolability of the dignity of every human being anchored in the German Basic Law and based on the experience of Nazi terror that cost the lives of millions of people, and in consideration of the positive experience of the reunification of East and West Germany as a result of protest movements that were anything but risk-free, representatives from politics, culture, religion, science, business and civic initiatives came together and, accompanied by the call "What unites us", formed an Alliance. Through discussion rounds, lectures, conferences, community fares and street festivals, concerts and art, the intention of the Alliance is to promote humane behavior, mutual respect and mutual acceptance. Against the backdrop of the peaceful civic protests that led to reunification, the "Dresden. Respect" Alliance is directed not least against a climate of exclusion and readiness for violence that is emerging in Dresden, and consciously opposes "arsonists, violent people and populists", their "cultureless demonstrations", their bawling and booing. In doing so, it advocates competitive discourse to the exclusion of all intolerance, as well as solidarity with people in need, characterized by humanity and empathy, and thus the realization of democratic postulates on the basis of the Basic Law. The events offered by the Alliance are characterized by openness to the world, interreligious dialogue, intercultural understanding, political and social participation. They oppose racism and misanthropy, and invite people to street festivals on Christopher Street Day, to public banquets and soccer matches. It organizes international weeks against racism, inviting all to join in song at Advent Singing in Zwinger, which already has 1,700 guests accepted invitations to the first event, and "to dance for more respect" (Das Volk tanzt—für mehr Respekt). The supporters of the Alliance are listed individually on the Internet. They are all united in not "talking about our differences for the umpteenth time" (Eva-Maria Stange), but to stand together against prohibitions of thought and speech, against attempts at social division, intolerance and disrespect, and to stand together for free democratic discourse.

BIRD e.V.

Already for years throughout Germany there have been cultural associations, which as music associations with the intended goal of integration also invite, in particular, refugees and immigrants to become a member. Because they are neither politically nor religiously oriented and, as such, are focused on unity versus internal distancing in terms of groupings, their integration potential is like that of sports clubs—a very special one, one that stands out from all other offers.

That they also exist in Dresden is, therefore, not what is special. What is special about a cultural or music association as a place of integration (here of BIRD e.V.), as a conscious union of people interested in culture, and those who create culture is the background of a special war history, the history of Dresden, and, more recently—besides the realization of a genuine, personal interest in music—in which many would like to oppose a populist, right-wing current, with a politically effective force.

Alone the names and the group affiliation of a small part of the active members of the association in the adjacent photo [Fig.3-46] simply demonstrates the diversity of the composition and strikingly conveys both its objective and intention.

Fig.3-46 Some of the members of BIRD e.V.: (from left to right) Heiner Dinglinger (Vietnamese Buddhist Cultural Center Saxony e.V.), Sebastian Römisch (Saxon State Orchestra of Dresden), Baljit Bulhar (Chairman of the Board of the Dresden Sikh Community), Johanna Stoll (Jewish Community of Dresden), Yusuf Sengun (Ditib Dresden), Amal Mitzscherling (Tom Pauls Theater Pirna), Adrian Zendeh (Bahai Community of Dresden), Roland Vetters (Elbland Philharmonic Orchestra Saxony), Prof. Martin Gillo (former Minister of Economy and Commissioner for Foreigners of the Free State of Saxony).

The association's program is unequivocal: "All people are first and foremost human beings, and only then members of different religions, world views, nationalities." Here and in the following, the homepage of the association serves as a central source of information. The program of the association can also be found as a central position in Liu and Spiegel: *Peacebuilding in a Globalized World*. As a Dresden initiative, it advocates a society "in which people of all religions and world views treat each other as equals." Regarding its specific objective, the association states on its website, "We support activities in culture and education of all kinds that show and strengthen the peaceful coexistence of religions and world views. We organize festivals, meetings and events that pursue these goals. We see ourselves as an initiator, multiplier and supporter of music and cultural initiatives for the whole of Germany and want to contribute in the long term to music and culture being recognized and used as a force to hold together the growing social diversity in Germany."

The members, who work on a voluntary basis, belong to various religions, including Christianity, Judaism, Islam, Buddhism, Hinduism, Sikhism and Bahaiism. They position themselves partly in pantheism and secular humanism. Their activities are intended to consciously demonstrate what "unites rather than divides" them. They understand their initiative as an invitation to join them in experiencing that beyond religious differences, peaceful coexistence "is not only possible, but enriching". The artists participating in the various events organized by the association want to demonstrate through their concrete interaction "that harmonious coexistence is possible and necessary across the boundaries of religions, world views, cultures or national origins." In this spirit, for example, quotations from the Holy Scriptures of six religions were read out during a celebratory concert in 2015, invoking universal peace and urging their followers to make it a reality.

In line with its objectives, the association also organizes "Interreligious or Intercultural Peace Concerts", "Interreligious Culture Festivals" and participates in the "Market of Cultures" in the neighboring town of Pirna. In addition, its event offerings include "International Weeks against Racism" or the exhibition "World Religions—World Peace—Global Ethics".

The "Third Interreligious Peace Concert", which took place in the Cross Church in Dresden with over 150 international artists, was held under the motto "Human First—United in Music". Among the renowned artists were a Kuwait-born conductor, son of German-Egyptian parents, a Vietnamese-German musician from Berlin, a Turkish tenor and the Middle East Peace Orchestra, an association of professional musicians, each with their own personal connection to one of numerous countries in the Middle East that are at odds with one another, and thus an ensemble that not only uses the "universal language of music", but also builds musical bridges between seemingly irreconcilable opposites in the best sense of the word.

Peace Work at the Dresden Environmental Center

It is not a matter of course that a cemetery invites people to work for peace and international understanding. However, this is exactly what is happening on the grounds of the Outer Matthew Cemetery in Dresden. Here the Dresden Evironmental Center (Dresdener Umweltzentrum e.V.) has not only received an outpost given by abundant nature, but also an obvious and comprehensible starting point for its own work. There are 207 Soviet citizens buried here [Fig.3-47], who died under the murderous working conditions in the armament factories of Dresden, or were killed in the air raids or in the war as members of the Soviet army. On the memorial stones placed here for Soviet soldiers, the names of the dead and their respective year of death in the period 1941-1945 are immortalized in Russian. Thus, each dead person is not only a lamentation and a denunciation, but also a reminder that everything possible should be done to prevent a repetition, not only in Dresden but also worldwide, of that which Dresden in the end was not spared, namely war, with all its faces of violence and suffering. The fact that the association has been doing peace work for years in an international network with Czech, Polish, Ukrainian and Chinese project partners fits in perfectly with its objectives. In 2015, it was also prompted to start working with

Fig.3-47 Memorial for Soviet victims of war

refugees. When Stefan Mertenskötter, an association member responsible for housing the site of the association on a cemetery, sees a connection between those who died in both world wars as "among us today" and sees himself prompted by those who have died from the war "to do practical peace work here in Dresden", then this view reflects once more the development of Dresden from a city focused on its own destruction to now assuming responsibility for an international collective for peace.

War and Peace in Pictures

It was a long time ago that Dresden was initially content to lick its own wounds. The photography exhibition "War and Peace" presented at three locations in Dresden documents that the narrow view of the February bombing and the terrible consequences of destruction associated with it in Dresden has broadened to an unlimited, expansive view of not only war everywhere, but war itself. One must even on the whole agree with Franz Kurowski, who cannot be followed in many remarks, with regard to the following summary: "Dresden itself is a reckoning to the spirit of annihilation, to war in every form; a demand for the ostracism of every aggressor. Dresden is a memorial of those tens of thousands who perished, and thus a memorial against war itself."

If war is reflected and thematized in Dresden today, then from a global perspective. Thus, the exhibition not only asks about the immediate effects of war, but explicitly about its aftermath, by creating access—via appropriate photographic material—to the worldwide round of wars in the time span from World War I up to current undeclared, asymmetrical wars. In this context, not only the snapshots of war, but also and especially the visible late traces that it has left behind in biographies and landscapes and, generally speaking, continues to leave behind, are of particular importance. Dresden in particular knows a moving song about these different periods of coping with and coming to terms with war experiences. Thus, the exhibition may give comfort, because it generalizes what Dresden has experienced selectively, but it may also cause despair, because it involuntarily makes war appear as an almost natural ubiquitous phenomenon. Of course, it intends the opposite: to make repeatedly clear the necessity of a protest against what the exhibition presents, the senseless death connected to war and its wounds that do not heal even after decades. The exhibition wants to rattle people by portraying the phenomenon of war from the perspective of war society. War traumatizes not only those directly involved in it, but also subsequent generations.

Peace March for Aleppo

For a long time now, the people of Dresden have not only been (pre)occupied with themselves, i.e. the collective trauma of the February 1945 bombing and its consequences, but have been able to classify this and productively process it not only for themselves in the larger context of war experiences worldwide, but also to make their experience and the way they deal with it informative and helpful for current war zones across borders. In this sense, it is also natural that a peace march [Fig.3-48] of over 3,000 kilometers planned from Berlin to Aleppo by around 100 participants from all over Europe will stop in Dresden to express their solidarity with the civilian population in Syria under the motto "Peace for Syria—Dresden Peace Demo"

Fig.3-48 Peace March for Aleppo

and to demonstrate for a peaceful conflict resolution in the war-torn country. Further stops on the march, which began in Berlin on December 26, 2016, were planned at that time for the Czech Republic, Austria, Slovenia, the Balkans and Turkey.

Dresden meets Aleppo (Manaf Halbouni), 2017

Often nothing is more welcome to artists than protests against their work. They want and provoke contradiction with the aim of stimulating reflection in and among those who, through thoughtless approval, support a status quo that the artists believe does not correspond to the given possibilities and, therefore, must be shattered.

The work of art by the German-Syrian Manaf Halbouni can also be seen in the horizon of this understanding of art. It is the upright erection of three disused buses on Dresden's New Market [Fig.3-49]. The background is that in the Syrian city of Aleppo, which has been considerably devastated by the war, three

Fig.3-49 Installation of the "Monument" in front of Church of Our Lady

buses served as protection for the population against sniper fire. The monument created by Halbouni—with it Aleppo was brought to Dresden and Dresden was connected with Aleppo—was criticized by right-wing political forces in Dresden with the argument that it disturbed the memory of the day of the "destruction" of Dresden (celebrated annually on November 13). The mayor of Dresden, who strongly welcomed the installation of the buses not far from Church of Our Lady, was even threatened with murder. The artist himself, since the installation of his artwork in Dresden from February to April 2015, protects himself against hostility by the greatest possible anonymity. The artwork was again erected a second time in November 2017 in front of the Brandenburg Gate in Berlin, where it was welcomed by the cultural senator of the state capital as a memorial to reconciliation and reconstruction.

Dresden Philharmonic Hall: Between War and Peace, 2018

If the abolition of war is a central objective of peace research, of which there is no doubt, then this aims at a condition through which it should be prepared to make itself superfluous, at least with regard to its bellicose orientation. Indeed, a commitment aimed at the prevention of war or its abolition only makes sense if it is carried by the conviction that this also serves the realization of its objective.

The pacifist goal and its corresponding undertaking could be opposed by views that understand war and peace as lows and highs of a pulsating movement. War and peace, one might infer from this view, "just happen" to alternate—as it were by nature and, therefore, basically inevitable. From the point of view of critical peace research, this assumption of a historically continuous coexistence of "war and peace" is not only an expression of a dangerous defeatism from a moral point of view, but it is also at the same time its breeding ground.

Conversely, ideas and representations of ups and downs of War and Peace do not simply lead into the marked field of tension. They also provide a critical view—just by naming or even describing the field of tension with its two poles and thereby, of course, making clear that (every concrete) war has an end one day and that this is followed by a period of peace. That, at least, may be comforting. And that is not nothing. Moreover, those who address the (constant) ups and downs of war and peace demonstrate by the very fact of addressing them that they do not buckle before the complexity of the questions associated with peace and war, even if they can only label them as a challenge, but cannot do justice to them in such a way that they even come closer to resolving them.

In an event of the Dresden Philharmonic exactly this and more than this happens. Norbert Schuster put it in a nutshell with regard to the event "Between War and Peace (Zwischen Krieg und Frieden) 1618-1918-2018" on November 10, 2018. It tells of the hopelessness and of being at the mercy of the individual, of the impossibility of escaping the barbarity of war once it is there. There is hardly any other way than to address the lamentation, but also the defiance against God or a supposed fate, and this on both sides of the front lines. The number of losers is overwhelming, the number of winners is small. Nevertheless, everything begins all over again, with new lies and new false promises. Breaking this vicious cycle is a hopeful vision—at the same time the task of all people, independent of the faith or worldview they may hold. Even though the event describes war and peace as a vicious cycle and its rupture as an innovation, it wants to encourage people to contribute to the realization of the breakthrough through their own commitment.

Human Chain for Peace

It is February 13, 2017, marking the 72nd anniversary of the bombing of Dresden in World War II. 12,000 citizens of the city of Dresden take each other by the hand on both sides of the Elbe and form a human chain [Fig.3-50] in memory of the destruction caused by the bombing in their city on the one hand, but also of the Nazi past of Dresden on the other. At the same time, with this action the participants, among them numerous families with children as well as members of the Saxonian state government, want to remind of the suffering of the people in the current conflict zones caused by war.

In the kickoff event for this, the mayor of Dresden, Dirk Hilbert, explicitly establishes a connection between the bombing of Dresden and current wars. In the horizon of today's globalized world, in his view, it cannot be ignored that numerous conflicts are being fought out in war and that human dignity is being trampled underfoot. Earlier, at a memorial stone in the central Old Market Square, he had already recalled, with the laying of a white rose, that after the bombing the bodies of almost 7,000 victims of war had been burned at the same location this event took place. In another event on the same day, the deportation of Jewish citizens of the city of Dresden between 1938 and 1945 was commemorated, and in the Tolkewitz Urn Grove, the murder of the disabled and mentally ill in Dresden during the National Socialist dictatorship. The mayor's statement that the Nazi Party was able to gather majorities in Dresden—"like in no other major German city"—and that Dresden was, therefore, not an innocent city in the time leading up to the Allied attacks, contradicts actions by right-wing extremists, neo-Nazis and PEGIDA supporters aimed at downplaying the Nazi Holocaust as a war crime with regards to the bombing of the city. Through baseless number games, these same right-wing groups attempt to place Nazi atrocities in the shadow of the Allied counterattacks in the course of instrumentalizing the Days of Remembrance.

Fig.3-50 Human chain for peace

Peace Academy of Church of Our Lady

Following its reconstruction, the architecturally unique domed building is not only a liturgical venue. Every year, well over 100 concerts and church music events take place in Church of Our Lady, and many brides and grooms say "I do" in it. "Church of Our Lady is a place of peace and reconciliation." This is the message that visitors should take in and carry forward. The program of the reconciliation stories made visible in Church of Our Lady and the peace work emanating from Church of Our Lady include, among other things, pointing out ways of working for peace, inviting winners of the Nobel Peace Prize to give lectures and organizing a "Peace Academy" [Fig.3-51] at Whitsun every two years, which usually brings together 400 young people from over 20 countries. Other focal points are the promotion of the "Cross of Nails" work initiated by Coventry (see above) or the implementation of the school competition "paxAN".

Fig.3-51 Peace work of Church of Our Lady—Peace Academy Dresden

Vigils for Peace Dresden

Every Monday at 7 in the evening a weekly gathering takes place at Dresden's Jorge-Gomondai-Plaza to exchange views about all conceivable matters of peace. The "Vigils for Peace Dresden" sees itself as a platform in which this exchange—as unideological as possible—is sought and conducted objectively and with mutual respect [Fig.3-52]. Unbiasedly, within the framework of an explicitly non-violent communication, peaceful ways of shaping the world are to be sought together. Participants register for speeches and counter-speeches on the basis of a tried and tested set of rules. Contributions that are contemptuous of humanity or glorify violence are expressly excluded. The platform does not provide a framework for racist, fascist or sexist statements.

Notwithstanding all openness, the vigil has agreed on a common denominator in terms of content. This includes, among other things, the demands for an end to any participation of Germany in war missions, as well as a general ban on arms exports and war missions of the Bundeswehr abroad, the exclusion of a drone war conducted from German soil, and the storage of nuclear weapons in Germany. In terms of content, the vigil positions itself against exploitation, lobbyism, corruption, and capitalism that is hostile to humanity.

Fig.3-52 In 2018, the "Vigils for Peace Dresden" celebrated its 4th anniversary

Recent topics include critical questions about the migration phenomenon as a phenomenon of exploitation and cause of momentous social deregulations, and about the membership of the Federal Republic of Germany in the North Atlantic Treaty Organization. The encounter with one of the last eyewitnesses of the Buchenwald concentration camp is another reminder of "War never again!" and a corresponding commitment. Another central concern is to point out the connections between capitalism and militarism and to oppose rearmament processes. A special commitment is the annual anti-war day, the International Day of Peace on September 21, in alliance with other peace initiatives in Dresden. In addition to public discussions, the vigils call for demonstrations and invite people to concerts.

Instruction at the Learning Site Dresden

On February 13, 2017, it was the 72nd anniversary of the bombing of Dresden, and with the publication on this topic. Even though it was more than seven decades ago, it still leaves no peace for the people not only in Dresden, but far beyond: that unforgettable bombing, and the numerous unfortunate victims. A school class, the 11b of the Graf-Stauffenberg Business School in Bamberg, accompanied by two religion teachers, set out as part of so-called archive trips or excursions to this memorable day to investigate the questions of peace and war as well as guilt and forgiveness in Dresden. Moreover, they did so in the contemporaneous field of tension between those who not only interpret the bombing as mass murder and a war crime, but who use it as such to minimize the war guilt of Hitler's Germany on the one hand, and between those who see in the attack (counterattack) on Dresden a consequence of their own war guilt and ask the former enemy for forgiveness on the other hand. In front of Church of Our Lady they not only encounter the memorial against war par excellence installed at this time, namely the bus action of the Syrian-born artist Manaf Halbouni, but also find themselves in a sea of lights of "hundreds of candles, another "memorial" against war. In an ecumenical service held in the Cross Church, they have the opportunity to meditatively explore the dimensions of reconciliation and peace. In the context of a church educational tour, which enables them to open up Church of Our Lady and its symbolic world in different ways, they are confronted with the testimonies of survivors—in the crypt and lower church of Church of Our Lady. In the peace work emanating from Church of Our Lady , the students see a good example of the church's social commitment [Fig.3-53].

Fig.3-53 Class 11b of the GrafStauffenberg Business School in Bamberg in front of Church of Our Lady

A current example from the field of contemporary art underlines the extent to which Dresden is striving to process its history in perspective, i.e. with a view to the future and that in a global sense by way of the arts. Henceforth, from February 5 to 16, 17 life-size angel sculptures formed of white concrete and attached to rollers, were on the move in Dresden's urban space as transcultural or trans-religious representatives of existential needs of joy, grief, hope, etc., known from religions and myths. The sculptures, created by artist Marit Benthe Norheim, were linked to a sound installation by Norwegian composer Geir Johnson. As shy, pregnant, but also wounded guardian spirits, they mingle with people and are close to them in their search for peace [Fig.3-54].

Fig.3-54 From left to right: Mayor of Dresden, Dirk Hilbert; Denmark Sculptor, Marit Benthe Norheim; Norway Composer, Geir Johnson; Director of Dresden Municipal Museum, Dr. Gisbert Porstmann

Conclusion

The fact that squadrons of airplanes equipped with countless explosive and incendiary bombs takes flight to drop them only a short time later over a city, is a crushing reality and demonstrates the capability and willingness of human beings to commit excess violence. In our textbook, we have dealt with the fact that this does not describe the inherent nature of a human being, but instead always the human being in a collective state of emergency. The personal readiness to behave violently in the context of a collective military act of violence is essentially founded in a stress situation, in whichever way it has come about, between or within countries and embedded in a corresponding propaganda and ideology, and often also in more or less long-term socialization and indoctrination processes.

From Dietmar Süß's broad perspective as seen from the views of political science, social history and cultural history, the extent of destruction in the bombing war between Germany and England is essentially based on such an unprecedented militarization of the population—with a strong combination of technical modernity and state disciplining. "War morale", as Ralf Blank summarizes a key research finding of Süß, "was considered social glue" by both nations. Weapons of mass destruction were ethically, religiously, and politically legitimized on both sides. Churches and ethical models of "just war" played no insignificant role in testing the ethical boundaries. As such, Süß breaks away from the narrow military-historical view of casualties and destruction and the often minute descriptions of battles and consequences, as well as lists of airdrop tonnages and the like. For Süß, air warfare is a "specific form of violence of modern societies in the 20th century".

When Christmas came and the soldiers could not yet return home contrary to initial promises and expectations, because the war, World War I, which began a few months ago, did not end as quickly as the warmongers had thought and predicted, the men in their trenches on the distant front in Belgian Flanders—German soldiers here and British soldiers there, often no more than 50 meters apart—suddenly became quite melancholy and began, hardly imaginable, to sing Christmas carols together across the war front. For a few hours at least, they experienced what—actually—connects them at the core: a life common to both of them as common soldiers of two hostile nations. Against the construct of a random nationality, a sense of belonging that was as strange as it was obvious rose up in them and brought them together for a moment. But for a moment at least, they touched upon their inherent reality: as people with the same basic needs and longings, with the same fears and hopes. When the British soldiers brought out a soccer ball and held it aloft, there was no stopping from the German soldiers either. The soccer match, which then took place on hard-frozen ground between the trenches and across all fronts, was rumored to have been won by the Germans. The next day, the same soldiers were again forced to kill each other. For the following Christmas, and several more thereafter, fraternization of this kind were strictly forbidden by the army commanders. Thus, humans may function 364 days in a year, on a single day, even if only for a moment, they become who they really are.

Late Triumph of the Peace Dynamic

It was the 60th anniversary of the air raid on Dresden, February 13, 2005, when Derek Jackson and Helga Sievers met in Dresden. He was just 19 years old at the time and one of those involved in the bombing by the British Royal Air Force. She was one of those who managed to survive the air raid. The fact that, after a relentless war and a long 60 years, they are now able to meet each other brings reconciliation to a focal point—in a way that they themselves and others had not been granted in the years before. This turns the widespread anthropological assumption that humans are naturally inclined to violence upside down. Here, in the eruptive, liberating breakthrough of humanity through the concrete blanket of ideology and demagogy, of propaganda, indoctrination and socialization, as expressed no more terribly than in war, the social microcosm celebrates against the social macrocosm, here David celebrates late triumph against Goliath. What is really human—however inconspicuous it may appear—is the state of reconciled togetherness. That we live in peace with each other, and that is what we strive for. Everything else is measured by this and is experienced as a deficit to be overcome.

When we wage wars, we know that this is not how it is supposed to be. Our standard is not war, but peace. It is Dresden in particular that, under the aspects of "splendor, catastrophe, and departure", brings home to us the fact that our longing for peace is an irrepressible one that endures all time, and that the peace dynamic hidden behind it cannot be stifled by any "event", no matter how terrible. Not infrequently, the destroyed parts of a city—after their reconstruction—shine in greater splendor than those not or only comparatively slightly affected by the destruction. Once again, life triumphs over death here in the end. That it can come to a lasting triumph, is the ceaseless, continuous task of the following generations.

Processes of Reconciliation on the Basis of Objectivity

That and how parts of Dresden were destroyed, the bare fact and the intensity or extent of the destruction—notwithstanding the fact that on the horizon of World War II they were preceded by numerous more than comparable destructions in other German cities and even more so outside Germany—have from the very beginning presented themselves as particularly extreme in every respect and have left their mark on the collective memory of a large number of people. The press, literature, and films, however, have done much to exaggerate the inferno, especially in terms of the number of its victims. For ideological reasons, the exaggeration in the historical revisionism of the right-wing as well as left-wing political camps has not only persisted until today, but for some years, against all better knowledge, has perpetuated, and one may even say: has been perverted.

Against this background, that Dresden has set out to finally—self-critically—examine the idea of destruction, which has solidified over decades and can hardly be surpassed, and the efforts it has undertaken to do so, is particularly remarkable. This would include examining the resilience of its individual assertions and thus credibility, and rejecting all distortions on the basis of results of scientific investigations, in the interest of a truth that is still terrible enough even with up to 25,000 bomb victims. Thus, it would readjust the German-British discourse on its own initiative. After the spontaneous offer of reconciliation from Coventry in 1946, this explicit will to objectivity is a late sign in advancing the reconciliation work, also on the part of postwar Germany by a differentiating view of the area bombing of Dresden. Exaggerations and distortions are counterproductive here. Only a most objective description of the consequences of the bombing and its placement within the context of the war overall will give those who deployed it, especially the British, room to partake in shaping the process of reconciliation. Participation under the condition of a polemically exaggerated framework can, therefore, be out of the question for those it pertains to, because they understandably cannot be prepared to take responsibility for an unreal scale of atrocities.

The Relevance of Education on Peace to the Culture of Remembrance

In medicine, it is customary to systematically record individual measures and their respective results, and to evaluate them in comparative studies that are as comprehensive as possible, in the interest of advancing treatment methods and the associated prospect of increasing therapeutic success. The science of history proceeds in a similar way and thus provides indispensable substantial support to other social sciences. It recounts and reflects on what has been remembered by drawing on the work of other disciplines. We remember, compare, and interpret processes not least with a view to optimizing our access to the world and its shaping.

On the horizon of these efforts, we locate the necessity to see, recognize, and cultivate remembering as an indispensable constant of our coping with life. We speak of memory culture and mean by this the complex effort to take a look at the past that is as unbiased as possible, although never objective, and to make it accessible on the basis of scientifically founded approaches to the regularities of our way of shaping the world. According to Christoph Cornelißen, in addition to specific historical events, personalities and politically relevant processes play a role. Private memories of individuals, social groups, and national collectives have no less weight than scientifically founded historical testimonies. Memories can be documented in texts, as well as in pictures and photos, in monuments and architecture, in festivals and customs, even in normative ideas, symbolism and myths. It is, with Cornelißen, about the "perception of historical contexts from a current perspective" in the interest of "the functional use of the past for present purposes, for the formation of a historically based identity".

"Everything is fluid." This is especially true of a culture of memory that sees itself as dynamic, in which retrospections and interpretations of what is remembered are constantly questioned, modified, and renewed. Memory processes conserve history but are ideally—at the same time—open to the future, creatively and progressively.

In a society open to the future, memory culture finds every support not only on the political level, but also and especially on the educational level, not least the school level. In this sense, the exemplary, critical handling of the bombing of the city of Dresden is a contribution to the culture of remembrance worthy of attention not only throughout Germany, but internationally, here with the declared goal of doing everything possible to exclude—in general—a destruction of this kind by all peaceful means available.

Dresden is not "just" another example, historically speaking, of the terrible results of military conflict action, one case among many, indeed countless, in (human) history. It is anything but singular, even if it may be felt as such by those directly affected and others as well. It is one example of the normal madness of war and its inevitable consequences.

However, even from a generalizing point of view, it makes sense to take a special look at the example of Dresden, like any other, and to give it a special significance by focusing on it specifically. In the end, however, under the summary conclusion, the example of Dresden, as an initially historical case among many cases, will also have to be understood, judged, and treated as an expression of a phenomenon, a socio-anthropological phenomenon.

The bombing of Dresden in February 1945 stands for war in particular and in general. In the course of time and the reappraisal of the devastating bombing, the emotional view of the particularity of Dresden, which arose from traumatic consternation, changed into a factual view of the generality expressed in the particularity of Dresden— the war as such, i.e. its causes and conditions as well as consequences. This gives rise to the hope that the lesson to be learned from Dresden will not only make war questionable with regard to specific situations and constellations, but will also call into question the sensibility of war in general and— by way of example—make a significant contribution towards rendering the institution of war taboo in the future.

If You Want Peace, then Prepare for Peace; If You Want Peace, then Prepare for War

When it comes to Dresden, the city's internal war chronology alone should be a peace education lesson par excellence, if one takes a look at the ruins of the Cross Church, destroyed in 1760 during the Seven Years' War, and next to it the ruins of Church of Our Lady, destroyed in 1945 by the February bombing. How terribly the images resemble each other. Yet the survivors always pick themselves up and rebuild what was destroyed—a vicious cycle of destruction and reconstruction against the backdrop of the principle that peace can be achieved through war, which is still as nonsensical as it is illogical today. Thus, not only the history of war in general, but the special history of war in Dresden once again leads to the old Roman principle "if you want peace, then prepare for war" (si vis pacem, para bellum) as absurdum and makes room for the only logical alternative, namely that peace can only be realized by the path of peace, so the context must be, following the Latin formulation: "if you want peace, then prepare for peace"(si vis pacem, para pacem).

Processing or Forgetting War Experiences

In this sense, peace education as a practice of system-transcendent peace studies—against the dull maintenance of a principle long and repeatedly refuted and the constant recurrence of its consequences, namely the vicious cycle of war and war itself—relies on a perpetuation of not forgetting. Like Nanjing, like Coventry, Warsaw, Hiroshima and many others, Dresden is a warning sign that the paths of violence, against all purposeful reason, lead to the dead end of violence. A legal reappraisal of the events on the basis of historical retrospection and an appropriate administration of justice, for example, within the framework of war tribunals, can have a healing effect on both individual and collective post-traumatic disorders. They are, as an opportunity for many, indispensable tools for coping with war [Fig.4-1, Fig.4-2].

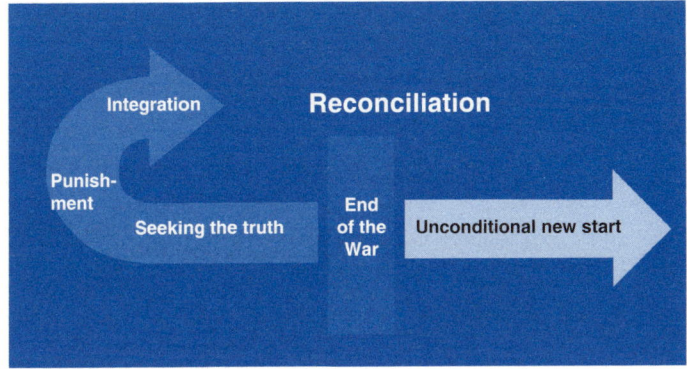

Fig.4-1 Reconciliation—two conflicting models:
The figure illustrates two extreme models of reconciliation: the complex reappraisal of war and integration after condemnation and punishment on the one hand, and the reduction of complexity through a new start in relations characterized by pure forgiveness on the other.

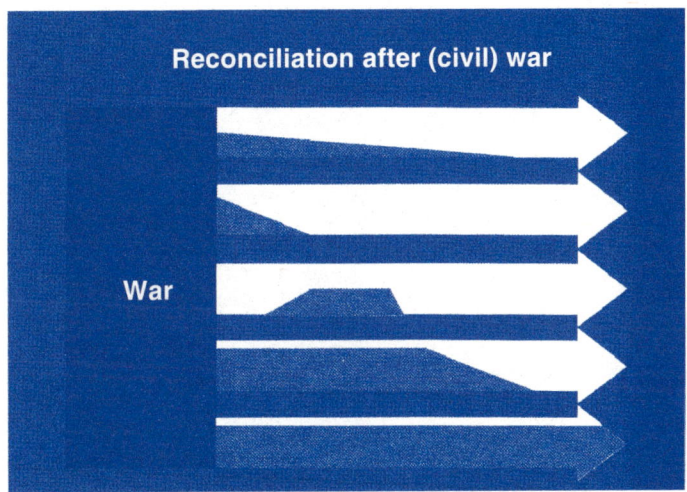

Fig.4-2 Diverse courses of reconciliation processes after war:
In the figure, the different courses of reconciliation processes after war are to be modeled: the dark color area in each arrow marks resentment, accusation and reservations, while the light area shows progress in reconciliation, communication and rapprochement.

Others flee from the problem into oblivion, most of them probably without being aware of the fact that this is also a reaction to an absolutely understandable existing traumatization and that such behavior does not help to overcome it conclusively. Regardless, they have the right of denial, the right to renounce retrospection. It is the generations following the war generation that often simply want to look forward and have little understanding for attempts to look back and lament the past and, on this basis, bring charges against whomever. In this way, they reduce the complexity of the war and use their limited energy in the interest of targeted contributions to the reorientation of their war-torn society.

This and similar photos can be found in large numbers on the Internet [Fig.4-3]. Young people have fun jumping from block to block on the Berlin "Memorial to the Murdered Jews of Europe". However, this is forbidden because it is too dangerous. The actual motive, however, is the possibility of irreverence expressed in it. The behavior of the young people, however, can also be interpreted benevolently as follows: the anthropological complexity of what the memorial stages can actually only be processed and endured by them by leaving the inconceivable crime, to which millions of Jewish fellow citizens fell victim, in high jumps underneath and behind them. This does not at all mean that it does not exist for them as a terrible fact.

Fig.4-3 Holocaust Memorial in Berlin

When a journalist once asked three young students, each respectively with Croatian, Serbian and Bosnian backgrounds, for their assessments of the war in Yugoslavia, he was met with incomprehension. Against the background of the differing views of their parents, who had taken part in the war decades ago, they preferred to forego their own interpretations and instead to see themselves as all ambitious students, oriented toward obtaining good degrees and a satisfying job, and to experience themselves, without distinction, as sitting in the same boat. All three were studying at the same university in Sarajevo at the time of the interview. They rely solely on their view of the future, which is untainted by any experience of war. Their partial forgetfulness of history fits into a promising globalization process. Nothing should be put in the way of young people, who with high and wide leaps attempt to transcend a history of total interpersonal failure, such as the Holocaust. They have the right to respond to it in this way, and to take on the future for themselves, to embrace it as light-hearted and with as much inspiration as they will. This does not preclude the acquisition of factual knowledge as part of their schooling, university studies or vocational training. In some circumstances, not in all circumstances, obliviousness to history in the form of emotional detachment is the best of all solutions.

The Long Shadow of War Propaganda and War

When I myself attended school, I was not confronted with even a rudimentary examination of the end of the German Empire (including World War I), the Weimar Republic, National Socialism and World War II during the 13 years of schooling, specifically from 1958 to 1971. This may be due to coincidences, but the school curriculum should have provided for the treatment of the historical periods. In retrospect, I allow myself to conclude that the older teachers were still so traumatized by the events that they were unable or unwilling to address them. The younger teachers, on the other hand, were not prepared, either through study or through internal social processes of coming to terms with the events, to deal with these pressing issues in a substantial way in the classroom. From a comparative historical perspective, I see this as a reflection of society's refusal to face the challenges of the recent past. On the one hand, there were so-called denazification trials after the end of the war, which is remotely comparable to today's truth tribunals, for example, in South Africa after the dissolution of the apartheid system and in Rwanda after the genocide, as well as the trials before the International Court of Justice in the Hague; in the well-known Nuremberg Trials, death sentences were even passed and executed on major war criminals. On the other hand, persons who played a not exactly insignificant role in National Socialism were able to continue working in comparable functions either immediately after the end of the war or at a shorter or longer distance from it. One of the best-known is the later Minister President of the state of Baden-Württemberg, who, as a naval judge, had recommended and passed four death sentences between 1943 and 1945. There were also opportunistic turncoats in the field of culture, especially in architecture and art, in schools and universities, and furthermore, of course, in the economy, simply everywhere. It goes without saying that those affected were not interested in coming to terms with the past and, therefore, did everything they could to slow down these processes, which were actually necessary. In moments of massive upheaval after war or revolution, the affected society is often interested in obscuring the past, even the recent past. It needs old leaders to still have a (reformed) function and so with renounces any research into these individuals. Only by coincidence and targeted reenactments do "brown" biographies come to light in individual cases. In the case of one of my professors, such a biography was discovered only after almost 40 years, after his retirement, and was uncovered amid considerable media interest. After the publication of the case, the significant course of an examination on the relationship between power and violence was explained to me. Here, the "brown" ideology broke through recognizably in a university lecturer, who was esteemed in general and also by me as a social ethicist.

It took a long time in postwar Germany and numerous interlocking processes of reflection and action to face the incomprehensible more or less self-critically. In 1965, against the mood in their own parishes, the Polish Catholic bishops wrote to their fellow bishops in Germany offering them forgiveness and at the same time asking for forgiveness. The German Catholic bishops responded by asking the Polish bishops and with them the faithful of Poland (more than 95% of the population) to forget and forgive. An important step was taken. The remarkable turning point, however, was the (spontaneous) genuflection of Willy Brandt (Chancellor of the Federal Republic of Germany from 1969 to 1974) in 1970 in Poland's capital Warsaw, 80% of which had been destroyed by the German Wehrmacht during the war.

The decision to go to war often takes only moments. Overcoming the enmities solidified or triggered by wars, dealing with the traumatization caused by them, and even more so the reconciliation processes indispensable for future coexistence often take many decades, not infrequently a century or more. Critical peace research is convinced that this must and can be put to an end. It works for this by showing, among other things, that war has neither the first nor the last word but has always been embedded in a much more comprehensive "peace", and with the help of the potential that exists within it, can not only be contained, but in the near future even abolished. "War is over!" Even if many see it differently, the signs of the times are focused on the abolition of war.

Main Bibliography

1. Backes, Uwe & Steffen Kailitz (Hrsg.), Sachsen-eine Hochburg des Rechtsextremismus?, Göttingen: Vandenhoeck & Rupprecht, 2020.

2. Baganz, Dorothée, Das historische Dresden. Bilder erzählen, Petersberg: Michael Imhof, 2006.

3. Bergander, Götz, Dresden im Luftkrieg. Vorgeschichte-Zerstörung-Folgen, Weimar-Köln-Wien: Böhlau, 2004 (auch als Sonderausgabe für Flechsig-Buchbetrieb, 2006), Erstaufla-ge ,1977.

4. Böttcher, Manfred Gerhart, Dresdens Tote. Die Totenzahlen der Luftangriffe auf Dresden am 13./14./15 Februar 1945. Vergleichende Studien-divergierende Ergebnisse, Frankfurt a.M.: R.G. Fischer, 2014.

5. Donath, Matthias, Architektur in Dresden 1933-1945, Dresden: Dresdener Verlagshaus Tech-nik, 2007.

6. Dresden-Memo (Spiel), Gedächtnisspiel mit Motiven aus Kunst und Architektur, Leipzig: E.A. Seemann, 2009.

7. Eckardt, Götz (Hrsg.), Schicksale deutscher Baudenkmale im Zweiten Weltkrieg. Eine Doku-mentation der Schäden und Totalverluste auf dem Gebiet der Deutschen Demokratischen Re-publik, Bände 1-2, München: Beck, 1978 (Berlin/DDR: Henschel, 1978).

8. Ellrich, Hartmut, Dresden 1933-1945. Der historische Reiseführer, Berlin: Ch. Links, 2008.

9. Evans, Richard J., Der Geschichtsfälscher. Holocaust und historische Wahrheit im David-Irving-Prozess, Frankfurt a.M.: Campus, 2001.

10. Friedrich, Jörg, Der Brand. Deutschland im Bombenkrieg 1940-1945, Berlin: Propyläen, 3. Aufl. 2002.

11. Fritze, Lothar, Die Moral des Bombenterrors. Alliierte Flächenbombardements im Zweiten Weltkrieg, München: Olzog, 2007.

12. Fritze, Lothar & Thomas Widera (Hrsg.), Alliierter Bombenkrieg. Das Beispiel Dresden, Göt-tingen: Vandenhoeck & Ruprecht, 2005.

13. Fromm, Erich, Anatomie der menschlichen Destruktivität, Stuttgart, 1974.

14. Grayling, Anthony C., Among the Dead Cities. Is the Targeting of Civilians in War Ever Justified?, London: Bloomsbury, 2007 (Deutsche Ausgabe: Die toten Städte. Waren die alliierten Bombenangriffe Kriegsverbrechen?, München: Bertelsmann, 2007).

15. Gretzschel, Matthias, Als Dresden im Feuersturm versank, Hamburg: Ellert & Richter, 2004.

16. Gründig, Claudia, Dresden früher und heute, Köln: Komet, 2015.

17. Hädecke, Wolfgang, Dresden. Eine Geschichte von Glanz, Katastrophe und Aufbruch, München-Wien: Carl Hanser, 2006.

18. Harwardt, Darius, Verehrter Feind. Amerikabilder deutscher Rechtsintellektueller in der Bun-desrepublik, Frankfurt-New York: Campus, 2019.

19. Hippler, Thomas, Die Regierung des Himmels. Globalgeschichte des Luftkriegs, Berlin: Matthes & Seitz, Berlin, 2017.

20. Irving, David John Cawdell, Der Untergang Dresdens. Apokalypse 1945, Gütersloh 1963 (Arndt 2006); engl: Apocalypse 1945. The Destruction of Dresden, Indianapolis: Focal Point Publications (Eigenverlag des Autors), 2007.

21. Kempowski, Walter, Der rote Hahn. Dresden im Februar 1945, München: Goldmann, 2001.

22. Klemperer, Victor, Ich will Zeugnis ablegen bis zum letzten. Tagebücher 1933-1945, 2 Bände, Berlin: Aufbau Verlag, 1995.

23. Kraske, Michael, Der Riss. Wie die Radikalisierung im Osten unser Zusammenleben zerstört, Berlin: Ullstein, 2020.

24. Kurowski, Franz, Das Massaker von Dresden und der anglo-amerikanische Bombenterror 1944-1945, Berg: Druffel-Verlag, 1995.

25. Lerm, Matthias, Abschied vom alten Dresden. Verluste historischer Bausubstanz nach 1945, Rostock: Hinstorff, 2001.

26. Moeller, Katrin & Burghart Schmidt (Hrsg.), Realität und Mythos. Hexenverfolgung und Re-zeptionsgeschichte, Hamburg: DOBU, 2003.

27. Müller, Rolf-Dieter & Nicole Schönherr / Thomas Widera (Hrsg.), Die Zerstörung Dresdens 13. bis 15. Februar 1945: Gutachten und Ergebnisse der Dresdner Historikerkommission zur Ermittlung der Opferzahlen (Berichte und Studien), Gütersloh: Vandenhoeck und Ruprecht (unipress), 2010.

28. Neillands, Robin, Der Krieg der Bomber. Arthur Harris und die Bombenoffensive der Alliierten 1939-1945, Berlin: Quintessenz, 2002.

29. Neutzner, Michael & Jens Herrmann & Arend Zwicker (Hrsg.), Gravuren des Krieges-Mahndepots in Dresden. Ein Kunstprojekt zu Dresdner Erinnerungsorten an Nationalsozialis-mus, Krieg und Zerstörung, Altenburg: DZA-Verlag, 2006.

30. Overy, Richard, The Bombing War. Europe 1939-1945, London: Penguin, 2013 (dt.: Der Bombenkrieg. Europa 1939 bis 1945, Berlin: Rowohlt, 2014).

31. Peter, Richard, Dresden-eine Kamera klagt an, Dresden: Dresdener Verlagsgesellschaft, 1949.

32. Pommerin, Reiner (Hrsg.), Dresden unterm Hakenkreuz, Köln-Weimar-Wien: Böhlau, 1998.

33. Quinger, Heinz, Dresden und Umgebung. Geschichte und Kunst der sächsischen Hauptstadt, Köln: DuMont, 1993.

34. Rudolph, Wolfgang, Feuersturm unbändiger Macht. Erlebtes Inferno-Dresden 1945, Münster: Monsenstein & Vannerdat, 2015.

35. Sächsische Landeszentrale für politische Bildung (Hrsg.), Unauslöschlich. Erinnerungen an das Kriegsende 1945. Ein Lesebuch, Dresden 1995, Dresden: Meissner Druckhaus, 1995.

36. Schaarschmidt, Wolfgang, Dresden 1945. Daten-Fakten-Opfer, Ares Verlag, 2018.

37. Schmidt, Michael, Der Untergang des alten Dresden in der Bombennacht vom 13./14. Februar 1945 / The Destruction of Dresden in the Night of February, the 13./14. 1945, Dresden: Son-nenblumen-Verlag, 4. Aufl. 2005.

38. Schmitz, Walter, Die Zerstörung Dresdens. Antworten der Künste, Dresden: Thelem, 2005.

39. Scholl, Inge, Die Weiße Rose. Frankfurt a.M.: Fischer, 1955.

40. Seydewitz, Max, Die unbesiegbare Stadt. Zerstörung und Neuanfang von Dresden, Berlin: Kongress-Verlag, 3., verb. u. erw. Aufl. 1956.

41. Slawski, Wolfgang, Mein Stadt-Wimmelbuch Dresden, Potsdam: Willegoos, 3. Aufl. 2017.

42. Soukup, Franz & Ernst Wrba & Franziskus Kerssenbrock, Dresden. Stolze Barockstadt an der Elbe, München: Bruckmann, 2. Aufl. 2017.

43. Stadtmuseum Dresden (Hrsg.), Verbrannt bis zur Unkenntlichkeit. Die Zerstörung Dresdens 1945, Altenburg: DZA Verlag, 1994.

44. Starke, Holger & Uwe John (Hrsg. im Auftrag der Landeshauptstadt Dresden), Geschichte der Stadt Dresden. Band 3: Von der Reichsgründung bis zur Gegenwart, Stuttgart: Theiss Verlag, 2006.

45. Süß, Dietmar (Hrsg.), Deutschland im Luftkrieg. Geschichte und Erinnerung, München: De Gruyter Oldenbourg, 2007.

46. Süß, Dietmar, Tod aus der Luft. Kriegsgesellschaft und Luftkrieg in Deutschland und England, München: Siedler, 2011.

47. Taylor, Frederick, Dresden. Tuesday, February 13, 1945, New York-London-Toronto-Sydney: Harper Perennial, 2005 (Deutsche Ausgabe: Dresden. Dienstag, 13. Februar 1945. Militärische Logik oder blanker Terror?, München: Bertelsmann, 2004).

48. Ulrich, Michael, Dresden-Nach der Synagoge brannte die Stadt. Dokumente, Berichte und persönliche Zeugnisse, Leipzig: Evangelische Verlagsanstalt, 2002.

For Photo Credits Please Refer to